Welcome to the *EVERYTHING*® series!

These handy, accessible books give you all you need to tackle a difficult project, gain a new hobby, comprehend a fascinating topic, prepare for an exam, or even brush up on something you learned back in school but have since forgotten.

You can read an *EVERYTHING*® book from cover to cover or just pick out the information you want from our four useful boxes: e-facts, e-ssentials, e-alerts, and e-questions. We literally give you everything you need to know on the subject, but throw in a lot of fun stuff along the way, too.

We now have well over 100 *EVERYTHING*® books in print, spanning such wide-ranging topics as weddings, pregnancy, wine, learning guitar, one-pot cooking, managing people, and so much more. When you're done reading them all, you can finally say you know *EVERYTHING*®!

E FACTS
Important sound bytes of information

E SSENTIALS
Quick handy tips

E ALERT
Urgent warnings

E QUESTIONS?
Solutions to common problems

THE EVERYTHING® Series

Dear Reader,

Working with dogs for more than half my life, I have come to the conclusion that they are truly one of the greatest gifts. Who but a dog would greet you so enthusiastically when you return home? Regardless of how long you left them, a minute or a week, you would get the same exuberant and ecstatic ritual as if the sun rose and set on your presence.

Your best friend and companion relies on you to provide an environment that is stimulating and interesting, to use training methods that are kind and effective, and to provide her with outlets for her boundless energy. The devotion your dog gives to you each day should be all the reason you need to search for the best possible training techniques and advice on her care. I hope this book will get you started on this journey, and that you and your canine companion share many happy years together.

Happy Tails,

GJB

THE
EVERYTHING®
DOG TRAINING
AND TRICKS BOOK

Turn the most mischievous canine into a
well-behaved dog who knows a few tricks

Gerilyn J. Bielakiewicz

Adams Media Corporation
Avon, Massachusetts

EDITORIAL
Publishing Director: Gary M. Krebs
Managing Editor: Kate McBride
Copy Chief: Laura MacLaughlin
Acquisitions Editor: Bethany Brown
Development Editor: Christel A. Shea
Production Editor: Khrysti Nazzaro

PRODUCTION
Production Director: Susan Beale
Production Manager: Michelle Roy Kelly
Series Designer: Daria Perreault
Cover Design: Paul Beatrice and Frank Rivera
Layout and Graphics: Colleen Cunningham,
Rachael Eiben, Michelle Roy Kelly, Daria Perreault

An Everything® Series Book.
Everything® and everything.com® are registered trademarks of F+W Publications, Inc.

Published by Adams Media, an F+W Publications Company
57 Littlefield Street, Avon, MA 02322 U.S.A.
www.adamsmedia.com

ISBN: 1-58062-666-1
Printed in the United States of America.

J I H G

Library of Congress Cataloging-in-Publication Data
Bielakiewicz, Gerilyn.
The everything dog training and tricks book : turn the most mischievous
canine into a well-behaved dog who knows a few tricks / Gerilyn Bielakiewicz.
        p.   cm.   —(An Everything series book)
ISBN 1-58062-666-1
1. Dogs—Training. II. Title. III. Everything series.
SF431 .B44 2002
636.7'0887—dc21
2002008504

This publication is designed to provide accurate and authoritative information with regard to the subject
matter covered. It is sold with the understanding that the publisher is not engaged in rendering legal,
accounting, or other professional advice. If legal advice or other expert assistance is required, the services of a competent professional person should be sought.
    —From a *Declaration of Principles* jointly adopted by a Committee of the
American Bar Association and a Committee of Publishers and Associations

Many of the designations used by manufacturers and sellers to distinguish their products are claimed
as trademarks. Where those designations appear in this book and Adams Media was aware of a trade-
mark claim, the designations have been printed in initial capital letters.

Illustrations by Barry Littmann.
Interior photography by Karen Hocker Photography.

This book is available at quantity discounts for bulk purchases.
For information, call 1-800-872-5627.

Visit the entire Everything® series at everything.com

Dedication

I dedicate this book to my husband, Paul, whose love, support,
and encouragement have helped me achieve my dreams.

Acknowledgments

Thank you, Mom, for watching my sons (both under two years old)
while I wrote, making it possible for this book to become a reality.

Contents

Introduction

Training your dog is a way to bring about a line of communication, a common language that you will use to communicate with your dog for her entire lifetime. Whether you spend time teaching your dog simple obedience commands or complicated tricks, you will expand upon your relationship with your dog and build a strong foundation of trust. Developing a trusting relationship with your dog through the use of positive training methods will not only enhance the special bond that you share with your dog, but it will also make the quality of life you share all the better. I can't think of a more exciting adventure than to train a dog and learn how her mind works and how she communicates. I think that with practice you will find that dogs are wonderfully intelligent and have a great sense of humor. Having worked with dogs for more than half of my life, and having taught close to 2,000 people how to train their dogs, I can honestly say that training a dog is a trip you don't want to miss.

Training is a relationship, and like all relationships it needs to be maintained through lots of repetition and practice. There is no designated beginning or end to training since a dog is capable of learning throughout its entire lifetime. Initially, training involves lots of practice and will probably include attending classes to learn how to practice when surrounded by distractions. Eventually, you may not train your dog formally every day, but your dog will still be learning new things every day, and participating in that learning is what owning a dog is all about.

Behavior problems can be detrimental to establishing a relationship with your dog and keeping it strong, and I have addressed several of the most trying ones in this book. The solutions are simple and concentrate on rebuilding trust in your relationship with your dog while at the same time improving your dog's manners and comfort. Almost every behavior problem relates back to some need that has not been met. You will notice a pattern as you read about the solutions to each problem: A lot of dogs would not exhibit behavior problems if they got enough exercise. If your dog is experiencing a behavior problem that is threatening your sanity, consider increasing her daily exercise and see if this doesn't help alleviate some of the intensity of the problem. The topics covered in this book range from teaching tricks to solving behavior problems, and I hope it in some way inspires you to build a great relationship with your dog and have fun doing it. There is no greater reward for your hard effort than the loyalty and love of a faithful canine companion. Great dog companions—like great human companions—are cultivated, not born, by spending time together, learning about each other, and learning how to develop the strongest relationship possible. It is my sincere wish that this book will positively change the way you view dog training and enhance your relationship with your dog.

Chapter 1
Why Teach Tricks?

Teaching tricks is a must for every dog owner who thinks of their pet as part of the family. Training a dog is like any other relationship; it is partly about establishing rules and boundaries (what is and isn't acceptable), partly about teaching your dog what is expected of her, and partly about spending time together and learning to enjoy each other's company.

Training Improves Your Relationship

From the moment you bring your new puppy into your home, she is learning how to get along with your family, a species entirely different from her own. If your instruction is vague and inconsistent, her confusion about what is acceptable will manifest itself in undesirable behavior and mischief. If you spend time teaching her what is expected of her, you will be rewarded with a well-mannered pet that becomes a beloved member of your family. As I often tell my students, you get what you reinforce. If you pay attention to what your dog is doing right, you'll reap the rewards of a well-behaved dog.

Boston Terrier with Ducky

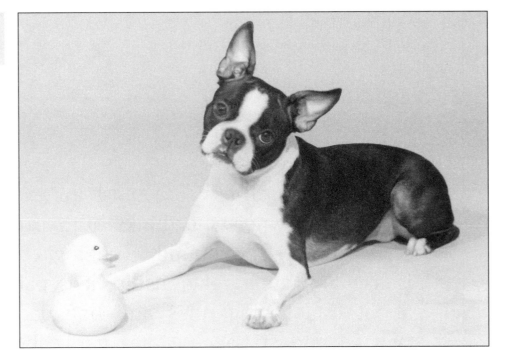

Teaching tricks is about having fun and being a little silly, but it can also greatly benefit a frustrated owner and an overactive dog. Teaching your dog to roll over, play dead, or sit may seem a bit frivolous until you realize that in order to do those tricks your dog must have some basic understanding of the Sit or Lie Down command. Teaching tricks capitalizes and improves upon what the dog already knows and makes it better. A goofy energetic dog will keep his paws off the company, for instance, if he has a show-stopping Play Dead command in his repertoire. Another benefit of trick training is that it improves public relations—doggie PR—with non-dog-lovers.

FACTS

Dogs that can perform tricks are perceived as friendly to most non-dog-people, which can improve a timid person's idea of your dog. What scaredy cat could resist a dog that says his prayers, rolls over, and plays dead?

The beauty of teaching tricks is that they can be taught to any dog of any size, breed, or temperament; you are only limited by the dog's physical ability to perform the task. I think it's crucial for larger dogs, especially those whose breed alone makes people nervous, to learn some fun and silly tricks that they can do when they meet new people. People will react totally differently to a big silly German shepherd balancing a cookie on his nose than they would to one sitting politely. This also has an added benefit for your dog: The more relaxed visitors are, the more your dog will like having them around.

Trick Training Leads to Better Training

Teaching tricks can help you control a dog that barks too much or shakes and shivers when she meets new people, by simply giving her a more acceptable alternative. Trick training will make you a better dog trainer, a person who knows how to motivate her dog and has learned how to break things down into small parts. Since training your dog is a lifelong process, the more you practice the skills of a good dog trainer the better you will get at it and the more quickly your dog will learn.

The most difficult part of being a beginner is that you are learning at the same time that you are trying to teach your dog. Be patient with yourself—dog training is a physical skill that requires lots of practice and repetition. You will reap the rewards a hundredfold the first time it all comes together and your dog performs perfectly.

FACTS

Performing tricks keeps old dogs young, agile, and flexible and gives young energetic dogs an outlet for their energy.

To teach tricks you will find you need to be able to break things down into component steps that are easily achieved in a training session. You will get really good at knowing how much information your dog will need in order to succeed at a given trick, and exactly when to fade out the extra help so that your dog can perform on his own. These skills come with time and practice, but there are several things you can do to help speed up the process.

1. Keep a notebook to record your training sessions.
2. Before you begin, map out the steps involved in teaching the trick.
3. Make sure you make your plan flexible, and be ready to add in more detailed steps if your dog has trouble understanding what you want.
4. Arm yourself with the best treats and rewards to keep your dog motivated.
5. Time your sessions; try not to make them longer than five minutes.
6. Read through the chapter on clicker training and be sure to familiarize yourself with how it works; it will save you tons of time in the long run.
7. Try to stick to the plan you've mapped out; don't click the dog for lots of different behaviors in one session.
8. If you get stuck on one particular trick, brainstorm with a friend about how to help your dog through it.
9. Add in distractions as soon as the dog starts to get the hang of what you're trying to teach.
10. Don't be afraid to go backward and review previous steps if your dog's behavior falls apart in a new place.

In general, being a good trainer is best indicated by your dog's attitude. If you keep sessions upbeat and fun, make it easy for your dog to succeed, and make sure that you end on a positive note, it won't be long before your dog thinks that working with you is better than anything else in the world.

The Importance of Consistency

Practicing on a regular basis is important if you want to become a good trainer and you want to accomplish the goals you've established for your dog. Designating a time to practice several times a week ensures that you will have lots of opportunities to experiment with techniques, and your dog will have lots of time to get the hang of working with you.

If you have a problem, or a new trick, success will come more easily if you block out specific times during the week and give yourself permission to drop everything for your dog. As you get good at including training in your weekly routine (or daily routine if your dog is young and learning the basics of living politely with humans), you will realize how easy the whole process is. You'll also appreciate how much fun it is to have a dog that works with you because she enjoys it.

Take a Class

Some people find it difficult to block out time for training; they need the consistency of being enrolled in a group class to motivate themselves to practice. Many training schools offer more than obedience classes; some offer agility classes, tricks classes, fly ball, tracking, hunting, herding, or other types of dog sports. Learning something new is more fun when you have the right tools and support—so be sure that the training school's philosophy matches your own and that you feel comfortable there.

ESSENTIALS As you search for the right dog-training school, remember that dog training doesn't require the use of force. If you are having problems with your dog's behavior, she needs more training, not heavy-handed corrections and reprimands.

Strengthen Your Relationship with Your Dog

When you are training your dog, you are teaching him to share a common language. Teaching your dog the meaning of the basic obedience commands gives you a vocabulary with which to communicate in day-to-day interactions with your dog. As with any communication, you and your dog need to understand each other. Once you find a way that works for you, don't change it. Otherwise, you'll confuse your dog and frustrate yourself.

Most people who train their dogs past the basics really begin to appreciate communicating with another species. Specialized training expands your bond with your dog and lets you communicate on a higher level. You will be amazed at just how intelligent dogs are and what can be accomplished through training.

The strong bonds developed through training carry over in play and in all the fun things you do with your dog. If your dog likes to swim and you like to walk on the beach, think of how much more enjoyable your time together will be if, when the walk is over, you can simply call your dog and leave.

Fix Behavior Problems

Teaching tricks can help you be more creative about fixing behavior problems with your dog. If you take the time to evaluate why your dog is doing what she is doing, you will figure out a solution that works for you. Some dogs that bark too much are quieter if they are allowed to carry a toy to the visitor. Dogs that jump can learn to do a Bow or Sit and Wave in exchange for petting from guests, or do their best version of Roll Over or Play Dead if you need to relax a non-dog-person who is afraid of your large dog.

Whatever the problem, use tricks in place of the inappropriate behavior to redirect the dog's energy and enthusiasm. The key here is to make sure that you practice the trick in all different kinds of environments with all different kinds of distractions until your dog's response to the cue is immediate and perfect. The more distraction-proof your tricks are, the more useful they will be to you when you ask the dog to do them.

Exercise for the Energetic Dog

You will find that dogs with lots of energy are really good at learning tricks. They offer a lot of natural behaviors that are easy to capitalize upon and turn into a trick. Little dogs love to stand on their hind legs or jump in place to see what's on the table, for instance, while big dogs like to spin in circles and stand on their hind legs to take a look out the window or to get your attention.

Self-Control

Training an energetic dog is fun because they don't tire as easily as other dogs, and they are always willing to try something new. An energetic dog will go along with just about any crazy trick you can dream up; they live for attention any way they can get it. Combining a romp in the park with tricks can give your dog an awesome workout and at the same time teach him manners and self-control.

ESSENTIALS

Teaching your dog simple tricks in one- to three-minute sessions several times a day can help alleviate boredom and create a more content dog. Giving your dog something to think about is a definite furniture saver, but it does not replace common sense about using gates, crates, and pens to keep your dog from getting into trouble in your absence.

Most people who own energetic dogs complain at some point about the dog's lack of self-control. Dogs don't just grow out of this; without training they will not one day wake up and act better behaved. If you don't put the time into training your dog to have better overall manners, you will live with a whirling dervish that never learns to simply hang out with people.

Know the Limits

Performing tricks requires some measure of control on the dog's part because she has to pay attention to your cues and get feedback on what's going right. Dogs that are constantly on the move need skilled trainers who can give them lots of feedback and break the exercise down into tiny steps. Trying to push such dogs too far too fast will result in frustration for both of you. Teaching a dog should be fun regardless of what you train your dog to do. The end result will be a dog that is an enjoyable companion and a treasured member of your family.

Therapy Work

If you need some good reasons to teach your dog lots of goofy tricks, think about the benefits of visiting nursing homes and hospitals. Share your dog's talents with patients who may have owned a dog at some point, but due to their health circumstances can no longer have a dog as a part of their lives. These folks might really appreciate the warm loving companionship of a well-behaved dog.

If you and your dog are visiting with patients one on one or in a group, use tricks to break the ice and to get people to warm up to your dog. Tricks are a great opening for conversations with patients and you'll often see everyone visibly relax and smile when they see your dog do anything remotely silly. I've found in all my years of visiting that the dogs don't have to do much to make people happy.

ESSENTIALS   Large and dark dogs can sometimes be scary to non-dog-people or children. What better way to introduce your dog to someone than to have him do a goofy trick that makes your visitors smile and relax. Play Dead and Roll Over are great for relaxing a non-dog-owning guest.

Trick training is something anyone can do and getting out there and showing people how much fun it is can be a great way to educate the public about the importance of establishing a relationship with their dog. Whatever the reason to teach tricks, the bottom line is to have fun with your dog. It is my goal in writing this book to get you hooked on training your dog! So why not find some tricks in the successive chapters and see how much fun you can have teaching your pooch something new.

CHAPTER 2

What's Your Dog Like?

Taking a moment to get an idea of "who" your dog is can help you design a training program that will be effective in teaching him to fit in with your family. Finding out how your dog responds to distractions and whether he's motivated by toys or games may be helpful in putting together a training program that is easy to implement.

How Well Do You Know Your Dog?

Breaking your training sessions down into small steps, finding out what motivates your dog, and finding out where your dog is most distracted will help you know where to start. Below are some questions you might want to ask yourself before you begin your training program.

- Is he energetic or laid back? A maniac retriever or a couch potato?
- Does he do something that you've always meant to put on cue but didn't know how to?
- Is his attention span short or long? How does he respond amid distractions?
- What is his favorite treat or toy?
- Does he give up easily or does he persist until he gets the job done?

Understanding your dog's personality and learning style is essential to enjoyably and successfully teaching him tricks, or anything else. Combining an energetic dog with a fast moving and flashy trick is exciting and invigorating not only for the dog, but also for your audience. Knowing your dog includes knowing what motivates him. Finding just the right kind of treat, toy, or game will help your dog associate training with fun and help your training program be a success.

Energy Level

Some dogs are couch potatoes; others run circles around us all day. Differences in breed, temperament, and personality all come into play when designing a successful training program. Living with your dog makes you the expert when it comes to knowing the ins and outs of her personality and just what will work for her. Paying attention to how active your dog is can help you learn about her personality and help you choose a trick that will be easy and fun to teach.

Highly Active

Active dogs love active tricks because they make the most of natural behaviors, such as spinning, jumping, barking, and pawing. When dogs have this much energy, take advantage of their abilities and teach appropriate tricks.

ESSENTIALS

If you are a beginner trainer and are having a hard time keeping up with your dog, don't be afraid to hire a professional trainer to coach you. The more skills you gain as your dog's trainer, the better you will be able to help your dog understand what you are trying to teach him.

However, high-energy dogs get overstimulated easily, and do best in short, concise training sessions with clear goals in mind. If you don't push a high-energy dog to work for long periods, they will fall in love with learning tricks.

Less Active

Lower-energy dogs may be harder to get moving until they figure out what you want them to do. These dogs are thinkers, and they like to know where you're going with all this. Go slowly with your dog. Try to keep your sessions short, because such dogs often bore easily and hate repeating things too many times in a row. Training before a meal (using unique treats as rewards) often perks them up and lets you get a good session in.

Medium-energy dogs are the easiest to work with because they allow you to make a lot of mistakes and be less organized. They don't mind repeating things over and over, and they are patient with you when you make mistakes or haven't planned out what you are trying to teach. Dogs with moderate energy levels are laid back and fun, turning their energy on like a rocket booster when they need to, but generally going along with whatever you're doing.

Personality

Ask yourself some questions about your dog's personality traits to discover where to begin your training program. It can save a lot of time if you start training your dog in an environment that isn't so distracting that he can't pay attention. An outgoing dog will love tricks that he can perform in a crowd, while a wallflower may prefer performing at a bit of a distance. Teaching your dog where he is most relaxed and least distracted, or worried, will help him be successful.

Social Temperament

A dog that is easily distracted by her friendliness around people will benefit from training sessions that start somewhere quiet, then quickly move on to involve the distractions she finds hard to resist. Training your dog to perform tricks around distractions from the start is one way to ensure that her performance will not fall apart in public.

Shy dogs, on the other hand, may resist doing tricks in public until they are more confident. With this type of dog, practice in the most comfortable environment possible, and then gradually integrate distractions with familiar people. The ultimate goal is to incorporate strangers and new places so that your dog can perform anywhere.

QUESTIONS?

How do you work with your dog around distractions?
If you can't get your dog's attention in ten to fifteen seconds, start putting some distance between your dog and the distraction. Increasing the distance will make it easier for your dog to focus and perform the exercise. As he gains confidence and learns to pay attention, you can then decrease the distance slowly without losing the behavior.

Special Talents and Interests

Depending on a dog's breed characteristics, he will often display a natural talent for certain tricks. For instance, Labrador and Golden retrievers often excel at tricks that involve having things in their mouths, like Put Away Your Toys or Go Fetch Me a Coke from the Refrigerator. Herding breeds might prefer to learn directional tricks like spinning to the left or right. A small dog that stands on its hind legs a lot may be a great candidate to learn Sit Up and Beg or Dance. A large-breed dog may be perfect for Play Dead, especially if he is of the low-energy mindset.

The most important thing to remember here is that any dog can master tricks that are physically possible for it to do. Dogs are amazing creatures, and they are so willing to be with us and please us that they will put up with a lot so long as they are getting some attention. With enough patience and practice, and the right training tools, you can teach your dog to do just about anything!

Keep Safety in Mind

Keep your dog's safety in mind while you are training, and pay attention to its physical limitations. If you have a long-backed breed like a basset hound for instance, it may not be a good idea to teach her to Sit Up Pretty, since her torso would be awfully heavy to support on such short legs. For larger breeds like Great Danes and Saint Bernards, you may not want to do any tricks that involve jumping, since the impact of landing is not good for their joints.

FACTS

If your dog refuses to assume a certain position, don't be afraid to have her checked for an injury. Dogs are stoic animals and rarely show discomfort unless it's obvious. Hiding injuries is instinctive, stemming from their wolf cousins who live by the rule of survival of the fittest.

Pay attention to your dog's weight, also, since extra pounds can lead to injuries. If you respect your dog's physical limitations, he will amaze you with his willingness to try what you ask. A dog cannot tell you outright if something is uncomfortable, so do your best to read his body language and go slowly. As often as possible, perform on a soft surface like a rug, grass, or sand, especially for tricks involving jumping, spinning, or rolling. Being mindful of your environment will minimize injuries and make your dog more comfortable.

What Motivates Your Pooch?

Learning what your dog likes as rewards is crucial to being a successful dog trainer. Many people are surprised to learn that dog cookies and dry dog food just don't cut it. Be creative in what you offer your dog as rewards, and keep the pieces tiny if it's food. Even a Great Dane shouldn't get a treat larger than ¼ inch. Keeping the treats tiny will ensure that you'll be able to train for a longer period of time, because your dog won't get full too fast. It will also help you not to add too many calories to his daily requirement. Think about cutting his daily ration back a bit if you've had an extra-long training session.

Lab Mix with ball

The reward is your dog's paycheck for playing this training game with you. It has to be something he's willing to work for, not simply something you want him to have. Some people have hang-ups about using food to train dogs because it cheapens their bond with the dog. They believe the dog should perform out of respect or love for them. Nonsense. Using food to train your dog is a way to get where you want to go. Training a dog with what he wants as a reward is both respectful to his doggy-ness and effective in the interest of time and resources.

Dogs don't perform out of love; their behavior or misbehavior has nothing to do with their love for us. Even dogs that chew the couch and bite the postman love their owners. But if you want that postman-biter to like the postman, you'll probably have to use a reward that the dog likes a little more than a pat on the head.

Dogs are motivated by and will work for food, just like people work for money. We all need money to pay our bills and live our lives; dogs need food to live and enjoy theirs. Many dogs eat out of a bowl once or twice a day for free. Why not take that food and train them to behave in a way that is acceptable to you? Once a dog is hooked on training and you have a good bond with her, you can use other rewards to reinforce good or appropriate behavior. Here are some yummy ideas for treats:

- Boiled chicken
- Boiled hamburger
- Popcorn
- Tortellini or other types of pasta (cooked)
- Bread (bagel pieces work great)
- Carrots
- Bananas
- Dried fruit
- Cheerios or other types of cereal
- Freeze-dried liver (found in pet stores and supply catalogs)
- Hot dogs (cooked)

QUESTIONS?

How does *random reinforcement* work?
Once your dog has mastered new tricks and behaviors, start giving him treats sporadically. He won't know for sure whether he's getting a reward, but he probably won't take the chance of missing one, either.

To prevent your dog from getting diarrhea, don't give too much of any one thing. As your dog starts to like the training game, mix in less desirable treats (like dog food) with the yummy stuff so that he never knows what he is getting. Random reinforcement will keep him more interested in the game, and let you accomplish more in each training session.

Other Rewards

Most of the time we use a food reward in training because it is quick and easy. In beginner classes especially, students use treats because there is a lot to accomplish in only one hour a week. If yours is a dog that goes nuts over tennis balls or stuffed toys, or he likes Frisbees or chasing a flashlight beam, use these rewards paired with the click (see Chapter 4).

Toys and games are a whole different category of rewards that may be exciting to your dog. If you find your dog likes games and toys, make your training sessions even more exciting by mixing them in with food rewards. Some sessions could be all food rewards or all toys and games, or you can mix it up and see what elicits the best response. When using toys as a reward, the key is to make the play part brief and fun. The game might last five to ten seconds, and then the toy gets hidden and you get back to work. That way the reward doesn't distract the dog from the lesson. Here are some ideas for nonfood rewards:

- A short game of fetch
- A short game of tug
- A short game of catch
- Hide a toy and go find it together
- A toss of a Frisbee
- Chase a stream of bubbles
- Lots of happy praise and baby talk
- Vigorous petting and happy talk
- Flashlight tag (have your dog chase the light beam)
- A stuffed dog toy
- A stuffed dog toy that makes noise
- A squeaky toy with an obnoxious squeaker

Dogs are affectionate animals, and anytime you spend praising them and showering them with attention is time well spent. Chances are, you'll get as much from the affection and exercise as they do!

Help Your Dog Like Other Rewards

Some dogs love toys and will happily work for a toss of the ball at least part of the time. Dogs who are not as crazy for toys can learn to like them if you work at it. It is worth the effort on your part to get the dog interested in varied rewards, because the more he finds rewarding the easier it will be for you and the more effective your sessions will be. Here's how to get started:

1. Hold your dog on a leash and tease him with a toy.
2. Throw the toy out of range and ignore his struggle toward it, but don't let him get it.
3. Use a helper to make the toy more exciting if necessary.
4. Wait patiently until the dog looks away from the toy and back at you.
5. Mark that moment with a click and allow him to go play with the toy as the reward (see Chapter 4).
6. If he doesn't turn away from the toy in about thirty seconds, slowly back up to increase the distance between the dog and the toy. Click and release him to get the toy when your dog looks back at you.
7. Repeat this with different toys and allow the dog to go play with the helper every once in a while.
8. The play part of the reward should be brief, about ten seconds.

This exercise should help you rev up a dog that is only mildly interested in toys. Warming him up this way is often a great way to start a training session—it helps the dog realize that it's time to work.

Exciting rewards are critical to an effective program. If your dog isn't turning himself inside out for the reward, find something he likes better. Don't worry if you just can't get your dog interested in toys; there is no crime in using food in training. Remember that your dog eats for free every day, so it's okay to make him work for it instead.

Reward or Bribe?

Using food to teach your dog to perform tricks is simple, fun, and effective. One problem many people complain about, however, is that in the absence of food the dog won't perform the behavior. That just means that you aren't there yet. If you use food correctly, you won't need to use it to get the dog to perform the trick; it will come after the trick has been performed. This is the critical difference between a reward and a bribe.

A bribe is something that causes a behavior to happen by enticing the dog. For example, your dog is out in the yard and won't come in, so you shake a box of cookies to bribe him in. This isn't really a bad thing, but it isn't training either. Bribing can have its benefits, however, when you are in a hurry and out of options.

FACTS

Be mindful of the difference between bribes and rewards; they can mean the difference between a well-managed dog whose behavior is dependent upon your attentiveness and her hunger level, and the well-*trained* dog that responds to cues immediately and reliably because she knows that the consequences will be good.

A reward, on the other hand, is something that occurs only after a behavior happens. A reward reinforces the likelihood that the behavior will happen again. For instance, you call your dog at the park and he comes to you; you offer a treat and release him back to play again. A rewarded dog is far more likely to come to you the next time you call than is a dog that is put back on leash and put in the car to go home. There are two types of rewards at work here: the food reward, which reinforced the dog for performing the behavior of coming back to his owner; and the consequence for coming back, which was that he got to go play again.

If you know your dog well—his energy level, personality, special talents, limitations, and motivations—you will be able to choose tricks that make both of you shine. Spend some time with your dog over the next few days and make notes on each of these categories. You may be surprised to learn how many things you assumed he would like that he actually doesn't. Adjusting your teaching style and training sessions can have a profound impact on the success of your training program.

CHAPTER 3

Give Your Dog a Job

Most animals have a basic need for food, water, and shelter, which we provide for our dogs with barely a second thought. The often overlooked needs that can mean the difference between a problem dog and a really great dog are exercise and mental stimulation.

Exercise First; Training Will Follow

Exercise is a crucial element in any training program, and without enough of it, no real learning will occur. A dog without enough exercise is like a child without recess. What adult would like to teach a math lesson to a classroom full of six-year-old boys who haven't been outside to play all day? Without exercise, your dog will be hard to teach because he just can't be still long enough to pay attention.

Dogs vary in their exercise requirements, but all need at least thirty minutes of running, playing, and interaction with you each day. The amount and type of exercise is dependent upon your dog's overall energy level. A Border collie or active young Lab will need one to two hours of flat-out running and active play, while a couch potato Pekingese may need only a thirty-minute romp. Yet, every dog is different, regardless of the breed and its stereotype. Ultimately, the amount of exercise your dog needs is whatever it takes to make her tired enough to be able to exist in your home as a calm relaxed member of the family. Following are some clues that your dog isn't getting enough exercise:

- She paces from room to room in the house.
- She hardly ever lies down, even when everyone else is relaxed.
- She whines excessively for no apparent reason.
- She barks excessively, sometimes over nothing.
- She digs, destroys, and chews everything in sight.
- She never stops jumping when there are people around.
- She runs away every chance she gets.
- She runs along the fence using any excuse to bark at passersby.

If your dog exhibits some or all of these symptoms, she could probably use more exercise and mental stimulation. Most people don't realize that leaving their dogs in the backyard for hours at a time is not a good way to burn off energy and not nearly enough exercise to make for a relaxed family pet. Most dogs, when left to their own devices, don't do anything but bark or dig or lay around.

If you are going to use your yard as a way to exercise your dog, you will need to go out with her and play games to burn off even a tenth of the energy she's got bottled up. Inviting neighbor dogs over to play, if your dog gets along with them, might be another option. All-out running, chasing, and wrestling is what a dog needs to do in order to be tired enough to be a good pet.

FACTS

Energetic dogs that don't get enough exercise are obvious; they exhibit their excess energy in excessive barking, jumping, and other unwanted behavior. If your dog has behavior problems, increasing the amount of exercise he gets can cut your training time in half.

Work Out Together

For dog owners with an active lifestyle, there are lots of ways a healthy active dog can burn off energy while accompanying you. Jogging, mountain biking, and Rollerblading are excellent ways to exercise dogs with boundless energy. Just make sure that you start off slowly and gradually build the distance. Also, pay attention to your dog's feet, checking them frequently for cuts and scrapes. Try to have him run on a variety of surfaces, since pavement is hard on a dogs joints and bones.

Dogs that participate in such activities should be at least one year old and recently checked by their veterinarian for potential health problems. (Just as it can with people, vigorous exercise can exacerbate certain bone and joint disorders.) A fit dog is happier, and you will find that he is more focused on whatever activity you are enjoying together, and he will be more likely to do it longer and without injury.

Dog Sports and Activities

The reason we get a dog in the first place is to enjoy their company and share them with other people. Depending on your dog's personality and activity level, you may consider participating with your dog in any of a great variety of dog sports or activities. Enrolling your dog in an agility class might be an excellent way to introduce both of you to something new while maintaining a good level of fitness. Agility is an obstacle course for dogs involving things to climb over, around, and through, as well as hurdles to jump over. The course is timed and dependent on you being able to successfully lead your dog through a maze of obstacles to the finish.

ESSENTIALS

In this dog-friendly age of ours, services like doggie day care, play groups, and dog parks are available to help us exercise our restless pooches. If you try to fit in more exercise sessions but just can't seem to put a dent in your dog's energy, consider doggie day care one or two days a week.

If you would like to be an active participant in your dog's exercise program, you will find that there are many canine sports that require you to be almost as fit as your dog. From fly ball to tracking to search and rescue, the possibilities are endless. If your style is quieter, you may consider a visiting-therapy dog program that allows you to go and visit a hospital or nursing home on a weekly or monthly basis. This is an excellent way to meet other dog owners and keep your dog's obedience skills sharp, because you will be using them constantly.

If you have a lot of free time and financial resources, you may consider becoming part of the growing search and rescue dog teams that look for missing people locally and nationally. No matter what your interest, there is a dog sport out there that you and your pup will both enjoy.

Games Dogs Play

Dog games are a great way to boost his interest in learning new things and strengthen your bond with him at the same time. Regardless of the game, the true objective is to make sure you both have fun. Keep the rules simple and easy to follow, and play often. Involve as many people in the family as you can, and see how much fun it can be to learn new ways of interacting together. Consider any of the following activities and games:

Play Fetch—a great way to tire out a tireless retriever. Use a tennis racquet to hit the ball that much further for all-out sprints.

Go swimming—another great way to exercise a very active dog. Combine it with some retrieving for a really exhausting workout.

Play hide-and-seek—an indoor rainy-day game may provide some dogs with enough activity to let them sleep the rest of the day. Also use this game to perk up your dog's recall and teach him that coming to you is always the best option.

Hide your dog's toys—he'll learn to use his nose to track things down *and* bring them back to you.

Learn a new trick—practice until it's perfect, then show off to your friends and family.

Practice Pavlov—set up a treat-dispensing toy, and show your dog how to interact with it until it pays off.

Whatever you do, be sure you are having a blast! Keep it fun, and keep the pace fast and interesting; you will see your dog perk up at the mere mention of playtime with you.

Provide the Right Foundation for Learning

Mental stimulation is the second-most overlooked need of problem dogs. Learning new things and solving problems make life interesting and give smart dogs something to do—and keeps them out of trouble, too! All dogs, regardless of breed or energy level, are intelligent and interactive creatures that love new experiences.

Dogs that are tied outside, constantly frustrated, and emotionally neglected may start off friendly and welcoming, but eventually become aggressive and wary of strangers. They have nothing to do, nothing to think about, and are absolutely bored. Dogs like this, even early in their adult lives (two to three years old), are hard to train. They aren't stupid or uncooperative, just blank. They simply do not know how to learn.

Lack of early stimulation and training makes it more difficult to teach any animal at a later date, because he has no basis for and doesn't quite know what to make out of the attention. It is possible to teach these dogs, but it takes patience, repetition, and practice. The training methods and tools described in the succeeding chapters will help you teach your dog anything you care to take the time to teach.

Teach Your Dog to Think

The training methods described in this book teach your dog how to think and solve problems, which is important for any dog. The techniques are commonly referred to as "clicker training," and are based in proven scientific theory. The rules and guidelines (see Chapter 4) will show you how to use this method to teach your dog anything physically possible. It is so exciting to see a dog grasp the concept of what you are trying to accomplish, and respond so well without needing any corrections!

Golden Retriever holding keys

All puppies should attend a well-run puppy kindergarten class that teaches you how to teach your dog the basic commands (Sit, Down, Stay, Come), how to walk without pulling, and to come when called. The class should also offer a playtime for dogs in the eight- to eighteen-week range, and should be staff-supervised so everyone has a good experience. It is crucial to the normal social development of your dog that she gets to play with other puppies and safe, well-socialized adult dogs on a regular basis. The more good experiences your young puppy has the easier it will be to teach her anything later in life.

FACTS

As you read and do research you will find that there is no one way to train a dog. As your dog's primary caretaker, it is your job to find the methods that get the job done without harm to your relationship. Find a trainer who emphasizes building your relationship with your dog.

A list of qualities to look for in your dog-training school is as follows:

- A limited class size with an instructor/assistant-to-student ratio of 1:6 is ideal.
- The age range of the puppies accepted should be no older than eighteen weeks.
- Handouts or homework sheets to explain exercises are important so that lessons can be shared among family members.
- The whole family should be welcome to attend. (If you include your children, make sure you bring along another adult to supervise them while you focus on training the dog.)
- All training methods should be positively based, ideally clicker training.
- Demonstrations should be given with untrained dogs to show the progression of exercises.
- Volunteers or assistants who help with the management of the class should be available to ensure that you get the help you need.

The best judge of a good puppy kindergarten, or any obedience class for that matter, is you. Ask if you can observe a class before signing up your puppy. Make sure the methods taught are kind and gentle, and that the puppies seem to be getting it. Go on your gut instinct—if you like the instructor and she seems like a person you can learn from, sign up. Train your dog; it's the nicest way to say you love him!

ESSENTIALS
If a method makes you uncomfortable, don't do it. If you're not sure if something will work but the technique won't do any harm, go ahead and try it and see for yourself. Your dog will benefit greatly from an owner who is committed to finding the best way possible to train him to be the best companion he can be.

Practice and Consistency Is the Key

As with anything in which you want to excel, the more you practice the better at it you will become. All training is a learned skill; the more you work with your dog, the more effective you'll be as a trainer and as a team. For example, the beginning trainer is notoriously stingy with rewards, and her timing needs some work. Through lots of practice, you will find and develop your own training style, discovering what works for you and expanding upon it.

Tons of resources are available, through books and online, that will tell you everything you'll ever want to know about behavior and training. Search for obedience classes in your area and keep at it. Remember that your dog and you are going to be together for a very long time, if you're lucky maybe even ten to twelve years or longer. Time spent teaching her how to learn will benefit both of you for years to come. Start your dog on the road to higher learning today!

CHAPTER 4
Clicker Training

Dog training has become kinder and gentler to both the dog and the owner. No longer is it necessary to use brute force or intimidation to force a dog to comply. Training any animal is about opening lines of communication and learning a common language. Clicker training isn't a gimmick or the latest fad; it is a scientifically based technique that utilizes the positive principles of operant conditioning.

The Kindness Revolution in Dog Training

Use clicker training to teach your dog what you expect of him; it's an intelligent and overall time-saving endeavor. Positive reinforcement through the use of treats and a clicker will help you teach your dog to think. The old style of training—making the dog "obey"—is not only outdated, it also does not evolve his problem-solving skills or intelligence.

Training your dog with treats and a clicker is the fastest, most reliable way to train your dog and have fun while you are doing it. There is no need to coerce, push, or shove to get what you want; once your dog knows how to learn, you will have a willing partner and a better overall relationship. Hundreds of families have learned to train their dogs with a clicker and treats, and have enjoyed the learning process so much that they have come back again and again for more advanced classes.

FACTS

Animals in zoos, aquariums, and circuses have been trained operantly using positive reinforcement for decades. Can you picture putting a training collar on a killer whale and trying to make it jump? Just because you can force dogs to obey doesn't mean you should. Teach your dog to think instead!

The application of clicker training to dogs is pure genius; it simplifies and speeds up the process of learning for dogs and owners alike. Handlers of any age or size can learn the principles of clicker training, and since it is not dependent on corrections or physical manipulation, the size, strength, and stamina of the handler doesn't matter.

Getting Started with a Clicker

The clicker is a small plastic box with a metal tab that makes a clicking sound when you push down with your thumb. The sound of the click is paired with a food reward by clicking the clicker and giving the dog a treat. After a few repetitions the dog learns to associate the sound of the clicker with a food reward.

Why It Works

The click marks the desired behavior to identify for the dog which behavior earned the reward. Because the food is removed by a step—you click first and then treat—you will find that your dog will work for the sound of the click rather than just a food reward. By pairing the clicker with a food reward we have created a powerful way to communicate to our dogs what behaviors are rewardable. This comes in handy, especially with a very active dog, because it gives you a way to specify to the dog exactly which of the behaviors earned the reward.

ESSENTIALS

Starting with food rewards is faster than using toys and games. Once the dog begins to understand clicker training and how the game works, you can use other rewards, including balls, tug toys, or playtime with other dogs.

Think of the click as a snapshot of what the dog is doing at the exact moment he is doing it. The click clearly identifies for the dog which behavior is being rewarded. Not only does this make it easier for the dog to understand what he is doing right, but it also gets him excited about the learning process since it gives him the responsibility of making the click happen.

The Clicker As an Event Marker

The sound of the click is unique, like nothing that the dog has ever heard, which is part of the key to its success in shaping behavior. People often ask about using their voice instead of the clicker to mark the behavior they are looking for. In the initial stages of training your voice is not a good event marker because you talk to your dog all the time, so your voice lacks the startling effect that the clicker invokes. The clicker's uniqueness reaches the part of the brain that is also responsible for the fight-or-flight response. In short, it really captures the dog's attention.

The process of shaping is what clicker training is all about. Shaping is useful in all types of training, but it is crucial in teaching tricks. Shaping behavior helps the dog learn how to think about what they did to earn the reward. By not helping him or physically manipulating his body, you help your dog learn faster and more permanently by trial and error. Just like the jumping killer whale in the previous section, clicking, or its absence, indicates which behaviors will be rewarded and which will not.

ESSENTIALS

Once the dog has the idea that a treat follows each click, it is a good idea to remove the treats from your person and put them on a table, chair, or step. The dog will still get the treat after being clicked for the right behavior, but the treat will no longer be in your hand or pocket. This exercise will teach your dog to pay attention to the click, not the presence of the treat.

Shaping

Shaping behavior means breaking it down into steps that progress toward an end goal. Shaping is not a rigid list of steps, but rather a general guide to get from point A to point B with lots of room for variation, intuition, rapid progress (skipping steps), or reviewing if the steps are too big.

Prompted and Free Shaping

Shaping can be either prompted, using a food lure or target, or free shaped. Free shaping requires waiting for the dog to offer desired actions on his own, then rewarding him with a treat in order to capture the small steps of behavior that lead toward the end goal. Each trick you learn here will be broken down into its component parts. You can then embellish upon those steps if your dog needs things broken down further.

FACTS

Training a behavior is not always a process that moves in one direction. Don't ever be afraid to quit a training session and go back to it later with a better plan and a fresh mind. Sometimes the best way to move forward is to take a rest.

Keep notes on each trick you teach, and whether your dog is catching on to the components as presented or needs more explicit direction. You will find that detailed notes make it easy to pick up where you left off, and your training sessions will be more productive overall. You will reach your goals faster if you have a plan.

ESSENTIALS

Free shaping is definitely worth adding to your bag of tricks in order to give you lots of options in explaining what you want your dog to do. You just show up with your clicker and treats, and click and treat what you like and ignore what you don't.

For behaviors that involve natural talents or unusual behaviors, free shaping is the way to go. Because the dog is fully in charge of which behaviors she is offering, she will often learn faster (in some situations) and retain more than when you prompt her behavior with a lure or target. Free shaping can be time consuming however, since it depends upon the dog offering behavior, and requires patience on the handler's part.

Working Through a Shaping Plan

Teaching a dog that likes to jump on guests to Sit instead is a lot more complicated than teaching just a Sit/Stay. The reason for this is due to all the distractions and variables during any given greeting. Though a dog may be able to Sit when there are no distractions, this doesn't mean he'll be able to Sit when a kid with a hot dog approaches him or when he sees his favorite person. Dogs need to be taught how to Sit and Stay around gradually more stimulating distractions; they don't automatically generalize their behavior to all environments.

Teaching your dog to Sit instead of jumping requires that you break sitting down into small steps that are easy for the dog to accomplish but at the same time introduce challenging distractions slowly so as to maintain the right behavior. The steps to teach Sit/Stay around distractions are as follows:

1. Teach your dog to Sit by luring her with a treat, then clicking and treating her when her bottom hits the floor.
2. Once your dog is performing this well, delay the click by counting to two before you click and treat. This is the beginning of a mini-Stay.
3. Increase the amount of seconds between the time your dog sits and the click and treat until your dog is holding the Sit behavior for ten seconds at a time.
4. Once your dog can hold the Sit for ten seconds between clicks and treats, go ahead and verbally label the behavior Stay and include a hand signal if desired.
5. Help your dog generalize this behavior by going somewhere new or adding in distractions. You may have to lower your standards and start from the beginning until your dog learns to block out the distractions and pay attention to you instead.
6. Add in people approaching your dog from the side and not making eye contact.
7. Add in people approaching your dog from the front and looking at him.
8. Add in people petting her or talking to her.
9. Continue to change the variables until your dog will hold the Sit/Stay position regardless of the distraction.
10. As your dog starts to be able to handle the distractions and works longer and more consistently, wean her off the clicker and treats so that she will perform the behavior for the reward of being able to greet the person.

ALERT

Dogs are not good at generalizing their behavior; they don't automatically transfer it to other surroundings. A dog will Sit in the kitchen on the first try, but never Sit at the pet store or the park. If you want to have control over your dog's behavior anywhere, you have to train everywhere.

Using this shaping plan, you can teach your dog to sit regardless of what is happening in the environment, or who she is greeting. A less formal way to teach the same thing is listed below; you might try both shaping plans to see which one is more suited to your training style. The following shaping plan does not help the dog by luring him with a treat when he makes the wrong decision. Instead, this shaping sequence lets the dog make choices. You click only those choices that lead toward the goal of sitting and staying.

Often the dog will revert back to old habits like jumping and whining. Simply ignore the things you don't want and the dog will soon realize that those behaviors are not rewardable and will start paying attention to only the behaviors he is being clicked for.

1. Start off by clicking and treating the dog for any behavior except jumping (standing, sitting, lying down, walking around) for the first minute.
2. The second minute choose something specific and click and treat him every time he offers it. You'll want to pick something easy, like standing still for one second or walking without whining, so that he can easily succeed.
3. If you have an active dog that offers a lot of behaviors, you might want to limit his options by putting him on a leash and stepping on it so that jumping is not an option.
4. Continue working with the dog in short sessions until he starts to visibly startle at the sound of the click and holds the position for a second.
5. Next, withhold the click for a while and see what happens; most dogs will Sit out of confusion and boredom, and you can click and treat that.
6. As soon as the dog Sits (on his own without being prompted), click and treat.

7. Repeat this over and over and gradually increase the amount of seconds the dog has to hold the Sit for a click and treat, until you have the dog holding the Sit for a reasonable amount of time.

8. You can continue on this way to polish the Sit to greet visitors in any way you wish.

Regardless of which shaping plan you choose, you will see that there are times when things will go fast and smoothly, and you may even skip steps or make great leaps in your shaping plan. Other times you will come to a standstill as your dog gets muddled and confused about what he's supposed to do. You will need to re-evaluate your plan and break it down into further steps or help him out in some way. Learning how to shape behavior will make you a better overall dog trainer and make training your dog more fun.

Tools of the trade: Bit Bag, clickers, leash, and flat collar

Using Lures in Training

A lure is a piece of food used to elicit behavior. Its goal is to help the dog get into the right position in order to earn the click and treat. In beginning your career as a dog trainer it is often frustrating and time consuming to wait for your dog to offer the right behavior, so the use of a food lure gets things going. The problem with food lures is that unless they are faded relatively quickly, the dog (and humans) become dependent upon them in order to perform the behavior. If lures are not faded, you will not have a trained dog that can perform behaviors on cue; you will have a trained dog that follows food.

As a general rule, lure the dog six times in a row. On the seventh repetition, do all the same motions with your body, but without the food lure in your hand. If the dog performs the behavior correctly, click and treat. If he doesn't perform the behavior correctly, go back and lure him six more times and try it again. This mini-drilling-session trains the dog on how to perform the correct behavior, and it lets you see if he understands what he's being clicked for.

QUESTIONS?

Do all dogs respond to lures?
For some dogs, lures present more of a distraction and a hindrance than help. For such dogs, you should skip the lure altogether.

Your goal with using a food lure is to help the dog into position six times in a row; then on the seventh repetition, try hiding the lure to see if the dog starts to offer the behavior on her own. When you take the lure out of your hand, you can start fading it gradually by putting it on a nearby table and running to get it after the click. The dog knows it's there and is excited about it but is not dependent on you waving it around to get her into the right position.

Using this method to wean your dog off of lures means that you get the dog to perform the behavior, click, and then run to get the treat. Doing this exercise will help your dog to learn that she is working for the click, and that the treat is an afterthought.

Targeting

Targeting is a form of luring, but it removes the treat by a step. It involves teaching the dog to touch his nose to an object. You might use this tool

THE EVERYTHING DOG TRAINING AND TRICKS BOOK

in order to move your dog or have him interact with someone or something. Anything can be used as a target, but the three main targets are your hand, a lid to a yogurt container, and a target stick. (You can buy a target stick online at ✐*www.clickertraining.com* or make your own out of a short piece of dowel).

Hand Target

The goal with using targeting is to get the behavior started but then wean the dog off the target so that he is performing the behavior reliably without it. The same rules apply to weaning off the target as with weaning off the lure; use it to get the behavior started and then wean your dog off of it. To teach your dog to target your hand with his nose follow these steps:

1. Hold your hand palm-up with a piece of food tucked under your thumb in the center of your palm. Click and treat your dog for sniffing your hand.
2. Keep the food in your hand for six repetitions and then take the food out and repeat, clicking the dog for touching his nose to your palm.
3. Have the dog follow your hand in all directions while you move around the room.
4. Involve a helper and have your dog target your hand and then your helper's hand for clicks and treats.
5. Label the behavior of touching his nose to your hand by saying Touch. (More on labeling follows.)
6. Try the trick in new places and with new people until your dog is fluent. Don't be afraid to go back to using food for a few repetitions if your dog falls apart around a new distraction.

Lid Target

On occasion, you may want your dog to move away from you to perform a behavior at a distance. In that case, it may be useful for you to teach your dog to target a yogurt lid with her nose. The steps for teaching your dog to target a lid are:

1. Put the lid in your hand and hold a treat in the center with your thumb.
2. When your dog noses at it, click and treat. Repeat for six repetitions.
3. Present the lid with no treat and click and treat for sniffing or nose bumping.
4. Label the behavior by saying Touch again just before your dog touches the lid.
5. Put the lid on the floor close by and repeat, clicking your dog at first for moving toward the lid and then for actually touching it with her nose.
6. Move the lid at varying distances until you can send her across the room to bump it with her nose for a click and treat.

Stick Target

Another variation of targeting involves using a stick as your target. The target stick acts like an extension of your arm and is useful in working with your dog at a little distance from you. The steps for teaching your dog to touch a target stick with his nose are as follows:

1. Put the end of the stick in the palm of your hand with a treat and click and treat your dog for sniffing or nudging at it with his nose.
2. Gradually work your hand up the stick and only click and treat your dog for touching his nose close to the end away from your hand.
3. Try putting the stick on the floor and only clicking and treating when your dog touches the ends.
4. Have your dog follow the stick as you walk with him until he's racing to catch the end of it for a click and treat.

FACTS

If your dog is doing a lot of mouthing of the stick, don't click until she does something more appropriate, like nudging it with her nose. Be careful to click only appropriate touches and ignore all others.

Paw Targeting

There are times that you may want your dog to interact with an object with her paw instead of her nose. Teaching your dog to target with her paw may give you another tool that you can use to help her learn whatever trick you are teaching. The difference between teaching your dog to target with her paw instead of her nose involves paying attention to which body part is hitting the target.

1. Put your hand or lid out for the dog to see, but withhold the click until she steps near it. Because you have already taught your dog to target with her nose, she may offer only this behavior at first. Be patient and wait for paw action near the target.
2. Withhold the click to let your dog know that you want something other than a nose touch and see what happens.
3. Make it easy on your dog by moving the lid or your hand along the floor so that you can click her for moving toward it. An easy way to help your dog to get this behavior started is to put the lid at the base of the stairs and click her for stepping on or next to it.
4. When you withhold the click your dog may get frustrated, but don't be too quick to help right away; wait your dog out and see if she'll paw at the target or move toward it.
5. Practice a paw target separately from a nose target and be sure to have two distinctive cues for each one.
6. Frequent short training sessions will help your dog figure out what you want faster than long confusing ones.

For targeting to be useful, you must practice it often. The more experience your dog has with this method, the better it will serve you in your trick training.

Labeling Behavior

The major difference between clicker training and other types of training is that you don't label the behavior right away. The reason for this is that the early versions of the behavior are not what you want for the final behavior. The first click for heeling, for instance, is a far cry from what the finished behavior will be. Saving the label until the dog is readily offering the behavior will ensure that the dog connects its behavior with what is being clicked, first.

The label can come as a verbal cue or a hand signal or both, but should not be introduced until the dog is offering a decent version of it. If you label behavior too soon you will get a wide variety of responses from the dog. Wait until the behavior looks close to perfect before labeling it.

FACTS

Asking your dog to perform a behavior assumes that she knows what the label or cue means. Follow the Ten in a Row rule before asking for a particular behavior. The dog should perform the behavior (without clicking or treating or luring) ten times in a row without any mistakes. If she doesn't have 100 percent accuracy, do more training.

You can call each behavior anything you want, just be sure it is a simple one-syllable word as often as possible and try to be sure it doesn't sound too much like any other word you use with your dog. Dogs pick up a lot from your body language and the pitch of your voice but may have trouble distinguishing between similar sounding words, like *no* and *go* for instance.

Weaning off the Clicker and Treats

The clicker is a learning tool, a signal that identifies for the dog which behaviors will be rewarded. When the dog is performing the behavior on cue and reliably (with 100 percent accuracy), he is ready to be weaned off the clicker and treats. The click and treat always go together. You shouldn't click without treating because the value of the reward marker, the click, will become diluted and less meaningful to the dog.

One way to begin the weaning process is to have the dog repeat the behavior more than once before you click and treat. This gives the dog the idea that he must continue to perform the behavior until he hears his click. The worst thing you can do when you are weaning your dog off the clicker and treats is to do it cold turkey. Getting rid of rewards and affirmation that he is performing the behavior correctly all at once is too abrupt, and will result in a frustrated dog.

The key to weaning is going slowly, getting the dog to perform longer versions of the behavior, or performing it in more repetitions successfully. The weaning process may be a good time to start introducing nonfood rewards, such as the opportunity to go greet a guest after sitting, or being released to go play with other dogs after coming when called.

The Last Word on Using Food

Eating is most dogs' greatest joy, a pleasure that you can use to help your dog learn appropriate manners and become a well-behaved member of your family. Regardless of a dog's preference for particular types of food, all dogs need to eat in order to survive. So, whether your dog is food oriented or not, every dog will work for food—you just may need to search a bit to find the right kind. What instructors love about clicker training is that it works for every dog.

ESSENTIALS

Don't use fattening dog biscuits as treats. When it comes to calories, one dog cookie is like eating a snack-size candy bar. Instead, use things like carrot sticks or soft dog treats cut into small pieces.

Clicker training is successful because the emphasis is on the click not the treat. Once dogs figure out the game, they love it and will gladly work regardless of how they feel about food. If you have a finicky fellow, try diversifying what you use as the reward and cutting back a little on his daily meal.

For dogs that like to eat, you may have the opposite problem: too many calories. Clicker training uses a lot of food rewards, but that doesn't

Golden Retriever waving

mean you'll have a fat dog. The size of the rewards should be tiny, ¼ of an inch or less, and can even consist of the dog's meals. If you have a particularly long training session, you can feed less food at the next meal or actually use the meal to train. The length of your sessions should be five to ten minutes maximum, so your dog is not going to be getting a lot of extra treats at one time. If your dog is on a special diet, consult your veterinarian and find out what food treats you can use.

The beauty of clicker training is that it teaches dogs to think. It is a kind, nonviolent way to teach a dog what is expected of her. It is also long lasting and easy, making it fun for the trainer and trainee alike. Enjoy using this method to teach your dog anything your heart desires, starting with some of the coolest tricks around!

CHAPTER 5
Dog Training Basics

The time you spend training your dog is critical to developing and fostering a relationship with him. Training in itself is a relationship because of the way you communicate with your dog and develop a common language of words and signals. Dogs that are trained to respond to basic commands are more fun to own because you can direct their behavior for a more enjoyable life together.

Invest in the Future

An untrained dog still learns things, just not necessarily the things you want her to know. Part of your dog's training and communication skills has to do with the structure you provide for her about what is and is not allowed. Putting in the time to teach your dog the basics around various distractions and in new environments is part of being a good dog owner, and will help you avoid future behavior problems. The better trained your dog is, the better relationship the two of you will share.

Leadership Involves Controlling Resources

Dogs are pack animals; they thrive on rules, consistency, and expectations. Setting limits about what is allowed and how you expect them to act is not only fair, but also essential to having a healthy, well-adjusted dog. Don't worry! Being a strong, fair leader is not about being physical with your dog. A true leader would never need to pin a dog down or give a harsh correction.

Leadership isn't about forcing dogs to obey. It requires you to provide structure and establish boundaries by controlling resources. The amount of time you spend establishing that you are the greatest person in your dog's life, the one who has the ability to give your dog access to all that is important to him, the more control you will have over your dog's behavior and the better behaved he will be.

ESSENTIALS

Leadership is about controlling access to the things your dog wants, including sleeping and resting places, food, toys, attention, access to other dogs, or access to the outdoors. It is about *you* being in command, not the dog.

The relationship between a well-behaved dog and his owner is one that consists of limits and rules about what is expected, as well as consistent training so the dog can recognize what is expected. Developing a relationship through training will mean that you will always have a way to communicate with your dog, and nip behavior problems in the bud or avoid them all together. Being a strong leader is the first step toward ridding your dog of behavior problems. Following are some guidelines on how to be a strong, fair leader.

1. Nothing in life is free. Make sure you give your dog a job. Make her Sit for dinner, Lie Down before doors are opened for her, etc.
2. Humans go first through doorways and up and down the stairs. This avoids escapes out the front door or knocking you down the stairs. Teach your dog to Sit and Stay until he is released through the door.
3. Down/Stay sessions for five to twenty minutes at a time help teach your dog self-control and give her a constructive job to perform around distractions and company.
4. No dogs on the beds or furniture. Young dogs should sleep in a crate or in their own bed, not in bed with you. Your bed is the highest, most special place in the house and should be reserved for you only.
5. Don't repeat a command more than once. If he doesn't respond on the first try, he does not get what you were offering.
6. Ignore your dog if she nudges you for attention. Leaders give attention on their own terms, not when their dogs demand it.
7. Ignore your dog if he is constantly pushing toys at you. Leaders initiate play and decide when the game starts and ends. This keeps a dog on his toes because he never knows when the fun begins.
8. Follow through. If you've asked your dog to do something but she does not respond, make sure you help her to get into the right position rather than repeating the command.
9. Provide consequences. Ignore what you don't like; avoid yelling at your dog for barking or jumping, for instance. From your dog's perspective, any attention is better than none, and speaking to the dog can often be mistaken for reinforcement.
10. Avoid punishment. Instead, teach your dog what you want him to do.

Because you control the things your dog wants access to, your leadership will help you build a strong bond with your dog, convincing him that you are the key to everything he desires. Strong leadership will give you the foundation you need to teach your dog how to behave appropriately and become a welcomed member of the family.

The Ten Keys to Successful Training

Throughout this book, you will learn effective techniques to ensure the success of you as a trainer, and your dog as a student. Most "keys to success" are universal, but it will be helpful for you to think of them in terms of your pet.

1. **Be patient.** All dogs learn at different speeds and often don't grasp concepts as quickly as we think they should. Be patient with your dog and help him to be successful.
2. **Plan ahead.** Set your dog up to succeed. If your dog isn't "getting it," the behavior probably needs to be broken down into smaller steps.
3. **Be realistic.** Don't expect your dog to perform a behavior in an environment you haven't taught him in.
4. **Be kind.** Use positive methods to teach your dog what's expected of him.
5. **Avoid punishment.** Harsh corrections have no place in the learning phase of a dog's development.
6. **Reward effectively.** Reinforce proper behavior with what motivates your dog. A pat on the head is nice but not necessarily what he wants. Remember that this is his paycheck: Pay up!
7. **Be generous.** All new trainers tend to be cheap with rewards. Reward correct responses often and don't be afraid to reward exceptionally good responses with extra treats, praise, toys, and love.
8. **Set goals.** If you don't know where you are going and have not planned out the session, how will you know when your dog's got it!
9. **Practice often.** Teach your dog in short frequent sessions.
10. **Stay positive.** Quit with your dog wanting more. An enthusiastic student is always an eager learner.

The simple truth of training dogs is that you get what you pay attention to. Set your dog up to succeed, limit his options, and reinforce what's going right. Soon you'll have a well-behaved dog that everyone loves to have around.

Teaching the Basics

Basic obedience is part of most tricks. The better your dog's response to commands like Sit/Stay and Down/Stay, the easier it will be to teach any trick, especially the more complicated ones. The basics of Sit, Down, Stay and Come are foundation material for most tricks covered in this book. If nothing else, having some knowledge of the basics will help your dog to relax enough to learn something new. Teaching your dog how to sit or lie down can help you position her for success. You can't just expect that working with your dog for a session or two will make her reliable around distractions and new people. If you want your dog to be well behaved and respond to your commands consistently, you must put in the time to train your dog.

Teaching Sit

Teaching Sit involves luring the dog into position before you click and treat for the correct response. Remember that when using a lure, it's important to fade its presence quickly to keep the dog from becoming dependent upon it (see Chapter 4). Fading a lure is an important part of making sure your dog becomes reliable, and is truly grasping the concept of sitting. The steps to teaching Sit are as follows:

1. Hold a treat slightly above your dog's nose and bring it back slowly over his head.
2. When your dog's bottom hits the ground, click and treat.
3. If your dog keeps backing up, practice against a wall so he can only go so far.
4. Repeat this until your dog is offering Sit readily.
5. Take the treat out of your hand and, holding your hand the same way, entice your dog to Sit. If he Sits, click and treat; if he doesn't, go back to using a food lure for six to eight more repetitions.
6. Once your dog is doing this reliably (follow the Ten in a Row rule), verbally label the behavior Sit right before the dog's bottom hits the ground.

7. Repeat these steps in various places until your dog is responding well with no mistakes.

8. Now, without a treat in your hand, ask your dog to repeat the behavior more than once before you click and treat. Start with low numbers of repetitions like two, three, or four Sits before you click and treat, but don't follow a pattern.

9. To help him generalize the behavior, start practicing somewhere new—the pet store, the park, the vet's office. Remember that forgetting is a normal part of learning and you will need to go back to helping the dog, with a treat in your hand if necessary, if the place you are working is very distracting.

10. To test your dog's training, try for ten in a row. If he gets less than 100 percent, go back to practicing before asking for the behavior in that environment.

If your dog fails the Ten in a Row rule, you need to help him for a few repetitions before he attempts the exercise again without help. Going back to the previous steps to help your dog get into the right position gives him information about what he needs to do to earn his click and treat and prevents him from getting confused and frustrated.

Teaching Sit/Stay

Miniature Pinscher being lured to sit

Turning the Sit into a Sit/Stay involves two processes: getting the dog to hold the position for longer periods of time (duration), and holding the position while the handler moves further away (distance). If you teach this behavior in two steps you will have a reliable behavior that is resistant to falling apart around distractions. The steps for teaching duration include the following.

1. Get your dog into a Sit and then count to two before you click and treat.
2. Gradually increase the time the dog has to hold the behavior by several seconds before you click and treat until you can build it up to ten seconds between each click and treat.
3. When you can get to ten seconds, go ahead and verbally label it Stay and give the hand signal (most people use a flat open palm toward the dog).
4. Increase the time between each click and treat randomly to keep the dog guessing as to how long she must wait for her next click.
5. Add in distractions, and start from the first step to rebuild the behavior of Sit/Stay around this new variable.

SSENTIALS
Try not to let your dog be wrong more than twice before helping him into the right position, lessening the distraction, or changing the variables. If your dog makes more than two mistakes in a row, you need to change something so that he can be right more easily.

The second part of the Sit/Stay command is for the dog to hold the sit while you move away from her. The steps for teaching your dog to hold her position relative to yours are:

1. Get your dog into a sit and take a small step right or left, returning immediately. If your dog maintains her position, click and treat. If she doesn't, do a smaller movement.
2. Gradually shift your weight, leaving your hands in front of the dog. Click and treat the dog for maintaining its position in front of you. Practice this gradual movement until the dog is convinced she should stay in one spot.
3. Increase the distance slowly and keep moving at first, never staying in one spot too long without coming back to the dog to click and treat. Standing still too soon in the process will cause your dog to run to you.

4. As you are able to cross the room with your dog maintaining her position, start to stay away a few seconds longer before coming back.

5. Increase the time slowly so that you are combining both the length of time the dog holds the position (duration) and how close or far you are from the dog (distance).

Teaching Down/Stay

When you are teaching your dog to Lie Down and Stay there for extended periods of time, pay attention to the surface that you are asking him to lie on. Make sure it isn't extreme in temperature, and that it isn't so hard and uncomfortable that your dog fidgets and gets up a lot because it too uncomfortable to stay down. Short-coated dogs are often very uncomfortable on hardwood or linoleum floors, and will learn to lie down more readily on a carpet or towel.

1. Starting with your dog in the Sit position, use a treat to lure his nose about halfway to the floor. When your dog follows the treat by lowering his head, click and treat.

2. Gradually lower your hand closer to the floor. You may need to go back to a food lure for a few reps if your dog seems stuck and won't lower his head any further.

3. When you get the treat to the floor, experiment with holding it out under your hand, or closer to and under his chest, and wait. Most dogs will fool around for a while trying to get the treat and then plop to the ground. When your dog goes all the way down, click and treat.

4. Repeat this six times with a treat, clicking and treating each time your dog goes all the way down.

5. Now, without a treat in your hand make the same hand motion and click and treat your dog for any attempt to lie down.

6. If your dog fails more than twice, go back to using a treat for six more times and then try again.

7. Take it on the road. When you go somewhere new or involve distractions like other dogs and people, the behavior may fall apart a bit. Don't be afraid to go back to using a food lure to show the dog

what to do and then fade it out when the dog is performing the behavior reliably.

Shetland Sheepdog puppy being lured into a down

Some dogs have trouble lying down and seem to get stuck in the sitting position. Here are some tips for dogs that get stuck.

- Practice on a soft surface away from distractions at first.
- Use novel treats that the dog loves but hardly ever gets.
- Use a low table, the rung of a chair, or even your outstretched leg to lure the dog low to the ground and under the object to give her the idea.
- Experiment with holding the treat closer to the dog's body and between the front paws close to the chest, or further away from her nose at a 45-degree angle.
- Avoid pushing on the dog to get her down. As soon as you start pushing and prodding, the dog turns her brain off and stops thinking about what she's doing, letting you do the work. If you want to teach your dog to think, don't push or pull her into position.

The most important thing to remember while training your dog, especially if you're struggling with a lesson, is to be patient and practice often. Short, frequent sessions will be much more effective for you and your dog than marathon sessions would be.

Dogs are impulsive and love to chase things that run. Always be cautious about giving your dog freedom in unfenced areas. Your dog may be the best-trained dog in the neighborhood, but if a cat runs across the street he is likely to follow. Use a leash on all walks on city streets and be cautious when allowing off-leash freedom.

Teaching Your Dog to Come

Teaching your dog to come when you call him has more to do with the status of your relationship than anything else you've done to this point. If your dog believes that you are in charge, he knows that you control everything good and that he must check in with you often in order to have access to the things he wants. Review the section on leadership earlier in this chapter and try to be diligent about becoming a strong and fair leader.

From a training perspective, the first thing a dog must do in order to Come is to turn away from what they want and look back in your direction. To teach a strong foundation for Come, follow these steps:

1. Start with the dog on her leash in a slightly distracting area, keeping her from the things she wants, and wait for her to look back at you, then click and treat.
2. Repeat this until the dog no longer looks away from you.
3. Change the distraction, go somewhere more stimulating, or go closer to the distractions and repeat.
4. If your dog doesn't look back at you in thirty seconds or less, move further away from the distraction until she will look at you within that time.
5. When your dog is looking back at you predictably, run backwards as you click and deliver the treat at your feet to encourage the dog to catch you.

6. As your dog gets good at this, wait until she is on her way back to you before you click.
7. Verbally label this behavior Come as your dog gets to you to eat her treat.
8. Change the distractions. Increase the intensity of a distraction by going closer to it or increasing the distance between you and your dog by using a longer leash.
9. If your dog doesn't respond by looking back in a reasonable amount of time, don't be afraid to back away from the distraction.

The trick to teaching Come is to set your dog up to be successful. Don't allow off-leash freedom if your dog is not reliable, and practice, practice, practice!! After establishing a firm foundation for Come on a six foot leash, you would then use a longer leash, and go back and review all of the steps from the beginning. Some dogs will make great progress quickly, and others will need you to go much slower so that they can be successful.

Gradually increase the length of the leash until your dog can turn away from what he wants (the foundation for coming when called) and come back to you easily. You would then progress to dropping the leash and letting him drag it, and eventually take it off while reviewing all the steps to teach come. When you first take off the leash, you may want to practice in a fenced or protected area in case you've hurried your dog's training and he runs off and won't come. This means that you need to back up a few steps and put the leash back on for a while.

Though the process seems a bit long and tedious, it is well worth the effort of having a dog that comes reliably when you call it. As your dog gets good at checking in with you, you can begin to offer real life rewards mixed in with treats, like the freedom to go back to playing with another dog, the opportunity to sniff a smelly spot on the ground or the chance to chase a squirrel. If these opportunities are given as rewards your dog will learn that coming to you and checking in on a regular basis is a very good thing. Regardless of how well your dog learns to come when called however, remember never to allow him off leash in unsafe areas where a mistake could cost him his life.

Minimizing the Cue

In early training, the original cue you use to get the dog to perform is overexaggerated. When the trick is polished, change the cue to something more subtle or change a verbal cue to a hand signal instead.

In order to change the original signal to a new one, the order in which you introduce the new command is very important. The standard practice for introducing a new label is: new cue followed by old cue. If you don't put the new cue first, the animal will ignore it and continue to respond to the old cue. You won't be able to get rid of the old signal unless the new signal precedes it.

Roll Over is a good example of a trick where you might want to abbreviate the original cue or replace it all together. When you first start the training, you'd probably use a full arm circle type of motion close to the dog's body to get him to throw himself over. You'd eventually want to shorten that to a slighter circular motion or even a closed fist.

FACTS

To replace the old cue with the new one, you'll want to present the new cue immediately before the old exaggerated cue. Gradually make the exaggerated cue less exaggerated until the new cue is causing the behavior to happen.

Make a Plan and Chart Your Progress

Making a plan means breaking down each trick into individual steps and tracking or charting your dog's progress—and stumbling blocks. Get in the habit of examining your dog's success rate and periodically re-evaluate your shaping plan, making adjustments as necessary. Use the Ten in a Row rule as a general guide. If your dog can repeat a step with 100 percent accuracy, you are ready to progress to the next step. If your dog makes a lots of mistakes or acts disinterested, break things down into smaller steps or change your approach in some way.

With each trick or behavior you teach, write each step down in sequential order and set small goals for each training session. Keeping your session short (less than ten minutes) with a clear goal in mind will help you determine whether you need to make things easier for your dog. A training log is an important part of a successful program, because your notes provide a bit of history on your progress. If you run into a snag along the way, you can review the steps where you were most successful, see what worked, and make changes so you can keep moving forward.

 SSENTIALS Whenever you are teaching a new behavior, click and treat your dog frequently. If you find that you are waiting around awhile for your dog to offer the right behavior, you need to break the behavior down into smaller steps. Be sure, as you teach each new command, that your dog has lots of opportunities to be right.

The Importance of Practice

Dogs learn things by repeating them over and over. The more you practice together, the better the dog will become at performing the behavior reliably and on cue. Dogs don't generalize well, meaning that just because they can Lie Down on the first try in the kitchen, doesn't mean they'll be able to Lie Down at the park or veterinarian's office.

The best way to ensure your dog's quick, reliable response to commands is to practice frequently in lots of different environments. The key to getting your dog to perform around distractions, like people and other dogs, is to introduce them slowly. Give the dog as much help as he needs to be successful. Dogs don't need to be corrected for not performing a behavior in a new environment; they need to be shown what to do until they can perform the behavior on their own. If you find the need to correct your dog, you haven't done a good enough job of setting him up for success. Go back to the drawing board and plan out your sessions again.

Working on the Quality of the Trick

Working on the quality of the trick is an important part of taking your tricks to the next level. The qualities of distance, speed, and duration will help you polish your tricks and let you expand them to more elaborate performances. Distance pertains to how far away from your dog you can be and still have him perform the trick; speed refers to how fast he can execute it; and duration indicates how long he'll hold it.

FACTS

The simple truth of training dogs is that you get what you pay attention to. Set your dog up to succeed, limit his options, and reinforce what's going right and you'll soon have a well-behaved dog that everyone loves to have around.

The key is to work on improving one aspect of your dog's performance at a time. For instance, if you want to teach your dog to wave to you at a distance, you would not ask him to hold the wave (duration) for any longer than he normally offers it. Similarly, you would not work him at a distance if you were trying to work on the duration of the wave. Separating these variables of trick training will help your dog learn faster, more consistently, and more reliably.

Distance

To increase the amount of space between you and your dog, you simply need to lower your standards for all other aspects of the trick except his ability to perform the behavior (however sloppy) at gradually increasing distances. Start with the dog close and reinforce him for gradually increasing distances. You will know if you have gone too far because he will make mistakes. This means you should shorten the distance to where he was reliable and continue more slowly.

Once you have him working reliably at one distance, go ahead and gradually increase it until you are satisfied with the performance. Don't be afraid to go back to the beginning if your dog falls apart and you lose the behavior entirely. If you go back to the beginning and start again, your dog will catch on more rapidly and give you an even better performance.

Speed of Execution

Golden Retriever holding a beach shovel

The speed with which your dog performs a trick refers to the time between the moment you give the command and the time the dog actually starts to perform the behavior. To improve your dog's speed it is helpful to pick a number of seconds in which he has to perform the trick and only reward those repetitions that fall within your time limit. Anything more gets ignored. It takes most dogs only a short time to realize that it is how fast they perform the behavior that counts. Don't forget that if you are working on the speed with which your dog responds to the command, you should lower your standards for other aspects of the trick.

QUESTIONS?

What should you do if your dog refuses to perform a behavior you think he knows?
If your dog does not respond to a command you think he knows, show him again, using a food lure or hand motion to help. Repeat this half a dozen times and then try again. Dogs that don't respond to commands may be distracted in a new environment.

Duration

This aspect also refers to time, but deals with the amount of time the dog must hold the behavior, such as leaving his paw up to wave, before you reward him. You can teach duration by delaying the click for varying amounts of time and only rewarding repetitions that are longer than average. As you increase the duration, go slowly so as not to lose the behavior altogether. If you increase the duration too fast and the dog no longer performs the behavior, go back to the beginning and start again. You will find that if you are flexible you will make an enormous amount of progress in a relatively short period of time.

Applying these tools as you go about teaching your dog any trick you choose will make it fun and interesting for your dog to learn them. Concentrate on teaching the basics using these common methods before you start teaching tricks. Having lots of options will make it more fun for you to train your dog and more fun for him to learn what you want to teach him. If you follow the simple plan outlined in this chapter for establishing yourself as leader and teaching the basic commands of Sit/Stay, Down/Stay, and Come, you will reap the rewards of a well-behaved member of your family.

CHAPTER 6

Kindergarten Tricks

Teaching tricks does not need to be a complicated task. Even novice trainers can teach a dog an entertaining trick, giving both trainer and dog a sense of accomplishment. The tricks that follow are simple and easy to teach, and are even appropriate for puppies, with their limited understanding of the training game.

Teaching Simple Tricks

Each dog has a unique style of learning, and it is your job as her trainer to find the best techniques to explain to her whatever trick you are trying to teach. The amount of sessions to learn one trick will vary according to the dog, so just know that as long as you are progressing from one step to the next, you are succeeding. Some additional things to keep in mind as you work on new tricks with your dog:

- Only introduce one new skill per session. Skipping around too much will confuse the dog and might discourage sensitive dogs altogether.
- Remember that the shaping outlines are building blocks toward an end goal. As with most goals, teaching a trick is accomplished by starting at the beginning with the first step and progressing through to the end by adding each step, one at a time, until all the steps come together to form a trick.
- Once you've established a few basics, it's a good idea to review previous skills or steps as a warm-up.
- Try to work in two or three sessions per day to see real improvement and accomplishment in a week's time, but there should be at least two hours between sessions. Dogs take time to process what they have learned and sometimes a rest gives them time to put more challenging concepts together.

You can teach the following tricks most easily using one of the three tools mentioned in Chapter 4—luring, free shaping, or targeting. You may want to review the basics often to reinforce your general skills before attempting to teach these tricks.

Polite Pawing

Many dogs can do these simple tricks with very little prompting because they already use their paws to play with toys or get your attention. If your dog falls into that category, teaching these tricks should be fairly straightforward.

Give Your Paw

Give Your Paw may be the most natural trick for dogs prone to pawing. However, it also serves as the foundation for other paw-oriented tricks, so master this one first. The shaping steps for teaching Give Your Paw are:

1. Find out what usually gets your dog to paw at you and use it to get him to do it. As your dog's paw is in the air, click and treat.
2. Repeat this fifteen to twenty times until your dog is offering his paw readily.
3. Now, leave your hand outstretched and wait your dog out; don't prompt him in any other way and see what happens. If he lifts his paw at all, click and treat.
4. If after a few seconds he does not lift his paw, go back to helping him for another ten to fifteen repetitions before you try again. You want the dog to understand that lifting his paw is what gets the click and treat to happen.
5. If you are using your outstretched hand as the prompt that gets your dog to give his paw, this can be turned into the cue for the behavior. Show your hand and click and treat your dog as he is stretching out his paw.
6. Add the verbal cue Give Your Paw when your dog is raising his paw to slap your hand on a regular basis.
7. Practice in different environments with various distractions, being careful not to overwhelm your dog. If the behavior falls apart in the new place don't be afraid to make things easier for him and help him out.
8. Avoid repeating yourself over and over; give one cue, wait for your dog's response, and click and treat. If your dog's response is not quick enough, go back to helping him for six to eight repetitions before trying again.

SSENTIALS

If your dog does not usually raise her paw, try teasing her with a really yummy treat in your fist held at about nose height, scratching her on the chest, or touching her toenails with your finger. Most dogs will respond by raising a paw, giving you an opportunity to click and treat.

High Five

The High Five is just a variation of the Give Your Paw trick with a few minor adjustments.

1. Teach your dog to target your hand with her paw for a click and treat (see Chapter 4).
2. Present your hand as the target in various positions until you can hold your hand up, palm facing the dog with fingers toward the ceiling. Click and treat your dog for touching your hand with her paw.
3. Practice this until your dog is quickly raising her paw when she sees you put your hand up.
4. Verbally label the behavior High Five when it is happening on a regular basis.
5. Add in distractions and work on having her do it with other people as well.

FACTS

Sometimes you'll want to use a different cue or hand signal than the one you started with when you are teaching tricks. There is an order that must be followed before your dog will perform the behavior on the new cue. You must present the new cue before the old cue or the dog will not pay attention to the new cue.

Wave

Teaching your dog to Wave is adorable and effective doggie PR because it gives him an appropriate way to greet people. Establishing an acceptable behavior, such as waving, is one of the keys to eliminating jumping. To perform this trick, the dog must raise a paw in the air while remaining stationary, which you can teach using a combination of targeting and shaping. The shaping steps are:

1. Start with your dog in a Sit/Stay and move a few steps away from him. Go back every few seconds for a full minute to reward your dog for not following you.

2. Standing in front of your dog, ask for his paw and click and treat him for giving it to you several times in a row.

3. Take a step away from your dog and ask for his paw. Click and treat the slightest effort to raise his paw without trying to move toward you. You may need to reward him for staying for a few repetitions before he'll remain in position and lift his paw.

4. As your dog raises his paw to place it in your outstretched hand, start fading this cue by removing your hand quickly. Click and treat your dog for swiping the air.

5. Repeat this step until your dog starts raising his paw when he sees your outstretched hand.

6. As your dog starts to offer swiping the air readily without moving forward, you can begin to verbally label this new behavior Wave.

7. Change the hand signal to an actual wave by changing the position of your hand from an outstretched palm to a waving hand. Offer the new cue (the waving hand) right before the old cue (the outstretched hand), gradually fading out the old cue until your dog is performing the behavior when you are waving at him.

8. Add in distractions and practice in new places until the behavior is reliable.

Calm Canines

Training involves many elements, but there are two things to remember. First, make the most of your dog's natural behavior, as the paw tricks demonstrate. Secondly, use training to elicit desired behavior, such as behaving in the presence of other people or dogs. The following tricks will help your dog remain calm, and will put your guests at ease, too.

Bow

Teaching your dog to Bow on command will not only make for a flashy trick but also may help you put a visiting dog at ease. Dogs invite each other to play in this position and it can be an excellent way for your dog to learn to make friends. To perform this trick, the dog starts from a standing position and lowers the front half of its body until its elbows touch the floor.

1. Starting your dog in a standing position, hold your hand below her chin (about 3 inches) and get her to touch your hand, then click and treat.
2. Gradually make it harder by placing your hand closer to the ground in increments of several inches each time. Click and treat your dog for making an attempt to lower her head further to touch your hand.
3. When your hand is resting on the ground, click and treat your dog for touching it with her nose without lying all the way down. If your dog continually lies down, raise your hand by several inches for a while before continuing on.
4. Make sure you watch your dog carefully and click and treat any effort she makes to bend her elbows.
5. Once your dog will lower her top half, start giving her less help by removing your target hand before she touches it.
6. Fade the hand target until she drops her head when you just begin to make the motion with your hand.
7. Increase the difficulty by only clicking and treating those repetitions where she lowers her head fast.
8. Increase the difficulty by increasing the duration (length of time the dog holds the behavior) by adding a Hold It or Stay command. To increase the duration of the behavior, delay the click by one or two seconds and gradually increase the time.
9. Add a verbal cue like Bow just before she performs the behavior.
10. Take it on the road and perform in new places.

FACTS

In order to make progress in trick training, you need to work at a pace where the dog is getting clicked and treated frequently. As you increase the difficulty of a trick, try not to let the dog make more than two or three mistakes before you show him what you want him to do.

Play Dead

Teaching your dog to Play Dead is a show-stopping trick that is sure to make even non-dog lovers sit up and take notice. This trick requires the dog to lay on his back with his paws in the air and hold it until released.

Shetland Sheepdog playing "dead"

1. Get your dog to lie down, then click and treat.
2. Use a treat to roll your dog onto his side, then click and treat.
3. Fade the lure by doing six repetitions in a row and then trying the seventh repetition without the lure, clicking and treating the dog for performing the behavior.
4. Reintroduce the lure to get him to roll onto his back, then click and treat. Fade the lure after the sixth repetition.
5. Go back and put all three steps together so that he performs them all in one continuous motion for one click and treat.
6. Fade the lure by working with food for six repetitions then without food for two repetitions. Go back and forth until your dog responds the same with or without food. Note: The way you hold your hand will become the exaggerated cue that starts the behavior.
7. Change the old cue to a new cue by offering the new cue before the motion you used to get the behavior started. Pointing your thumb and forefinger like a gun and saying "bang!" is very flashy!

8. Work on speed by only rewarding the dog for quick responses to the new signal. Decide on how many seconds he has to start the behavior and click and treat even before he finishes. Clicking in the middle of the behavior is what builds speed.

FACTS

Review Stay with your dog first; then gradually give the cue for the behavior at greater and greater distances, only moving further away if the dog performs the behavior reliably. Don't be afraid to do remedial work with Stay if the behavior seems to fall apart.

Belly Up

This is similar to the Play Dead trick except that it also involves allowing someone to touch the dog while she is flat on her back. Not all dogs are comfortable with this, so know your dog well before asking for it in front of strangers.

1. Have your dog Lie Down, then click and treat.
2. Lure your dog onto her side, then click and treat.
3. Lure your dog over onto one hip, then click and treat.
4. Lure your dog all the way onto her back, then click and jackpot (give a large number of small treats) the first time and quit the session.
5. Once your dog is rolling onto her back easily, fade the lure after six repetitions and see what happens. If the dog performs the Belly Up behavior, click and treat. If not, lure her six more times and try again.
6. When your dog is readily rolling on her back, call it "belly up" just before she offers the behavior.
7. Delay the click once your dog is in the Belly Up position by at first a few seconds and then more and more until she will hold the position for longer periods of time.
8. Add in touching her belly, and click and treat her for holding the Belly Up position while you do this.

9. Add in the distraction of strangers touching her belly, and click and treat her for holding the Belly Up position while being petted.
10. Take it on the road. Practice in new places with new people. Don't be afraid to help your dog into position if she gets confused in a new place.

Who Loves an Audience?

Although some of your training is behavior modification, some of it is just plain fun. Once you've trained a well-behaved, socially acceptable dog, let everyone in on the games!

Roll Over

Roll Over requires your dog to lie down flat on his stomach, roll all the way over, and get back on his feet. Though the concept is simple, this is not always an easy trick for your dog to perform. Long-back breeds like dachshunds or basset hounds may not be as good at this trick as other breeds due to the way they are built.

Dogs with long backs sometimes find it uncomfortable and awkward to roll over on their backs and then try to get back on their feet. Overweight dogs or dogs that have had back injuries in the past may also have difficulties.

Pay close attention to your dog to be sure he's not hurting or twisting his back. If, despite your best efforts, your dog refuses to get on his back, skip this trick and try another. Your dog may be sore or uncomfortable and this may be his only way to express it. If possible, teach this trick on a soft surface like a towel or carpet so the dog is more comfortable.

1. Get your dog to lie down with his belly touching the ground, and click and treat.

2. Use a treat or a toy to turn your dog's head until he flops over on one hip, and click and treat.

3. Use a treat or toy held close to your dog's shoulder to get him completely on his side, and click and treat.

4. Gradually move the treat or toy, while he's chewing on it, to move him onto his back and then eventually all the way over. This step often takes many attempts before the dog is comfortable enough to be on his back.

5. Click and treat small efforts to move toward the treat at first before you get him to move further to get his click and treat. If you make it too hard to earn a click your dog will quit on you and think it's no fun.

6. When your dog is rolling over easily, it's time to start fading out all the extra cues and make him offer more before you click.

7. Once he can roll over with just this little bit of help you can begin to verbally label this trick Roll Over. Whatever you are doing with your hand or fist could be a hand signal for the behavior as well.

8. Add in distractions one at a time and be prepared to help him complete the trick if he has trouble concentrating.

Spin

Spinning involves your dog turning in a complete circle in either direction. As your dog gets good at this, you can have her keep spinning until you tell her to stop. If you've tried to teach this trick using a lure or food treat, you probably realized how difficult it is to get rid of the lure. Instead, use targeting either with your hand or with a target stick to show your dog what you want her to do.

1. Use your hand as a target and with your dog facing you, get her to follow your hand a quarter of the way around, then click and treat.

2. Now, leave your target hand at the quarter-way mark and wait until your dog touches it with her nose on her own before you click and treat. Practice this until she's offering it readily.

3. Next, just before she touches your hand, move your target hand to the halfway point and click and treat your dog for following it, but before she actually touches it.
4. At this point, as you drop your hand she may spin the rest of the way around, but continue to click and treat for the halfway point in order to build speed.
5. Use your target hand to start the dog turning, but then pull it away quickly. Click and treat your dog for attempting to turn without the target to guide her.
6. Time the click so that you're clicking the dog for being at the halfway point.
7. Continue to minimize your target hand and click the dog for continuing to turn without your help.
8. Fade the target hand to just a motion to the left or right.
9. Fade the target to a simple left or right cue. A pointed index finger would be appropriate as a final signal.

Once you and your dog have mastered ten in a row, you can begin working on speed (see Chapter 5). Set a time limit in which your dog must perform the behavior, and click and treat only those repetitions that meet the goal. To train your dog to spin in the other direction, simply go back to the first step and work your way through.

Are You Scared?

This trick will put a smile on everyone's faces, especially children's. To indicate his "fright," the dog runs under a table or bed and peeks out from under the tablecloth or bedspread. The shaping steps for teaching Are You Scared? are:

1. Start with your dog under the table, and use your voice or a treat to get him to peek out. Click and treat.
2. Make sure you time your click for when he first pushes out from under the cloth.

3. Repeat this six to eight times and then try putting him under again and waiting to see if he offers peeking out on his own.

4. Once your dog has this part down, teach him to go under the table using a target lid (see Chapter 4 for teaching targeting with a lid).

5. Bait the target with a treat at first to encourage him to go under the tablecloth and click and treat each time.

6. Take the bait off the target but leave the target under the table or bed and send him again. Click and treat your dog for going under the table or bed after the target.

7. To get the peeking behavior, repeat the above step (getting him under the object) until your dog offers it readily and then delay the click. When your dog doesn't hear the click, he will probably come back out to see what's wrong. Click and treat him just as he peaks out from under the cloth.

8. Repeat this until he runs under and peeks out readily; then verbally label the behavior Are You Scared?

QUESTIONS?

What if my dog doesn't peek?
If you're having trouble getting your dog to peek because he runs all the way out from under the tablecloth or bedspread, it means that you need to click sooner. An early click will catch the dog just as he is emerging and give him the idea that peeking is what is being clicked.

Who's a Brave Dog?

This trick is similar to Are You Scared? except in this trick the dog runs around behind the handler and through his legs until she is looking up at the handler's face. The shaping steps to teach Who's a Brave Dog? are:

1. Starting with your dog sitting in front of you, use a target stick (see Chapter 4) to get your dog to go around you to the left or right.

2. Practice this until your dog will run behind your legs and touch the target for a click and treat.

3. Slowly move the target between your feet so that your dog comes between your legs enough to be able to look up at you.

4. Withhold the click after your dog starts to catch on to going through your legs and see if she will look up at you, then click and treat.

5. If your dog runs all the way through your legs, use the target stick to show her where to stop and click and treat her before she actually touches it.

6. You can label this behavior Who's a Brave Dog? by saying the label right before you give the cue that starts the behavior, like pointing or whatever you did to encourage the dog to go around you.

7. Slowly fade the target as your dog starts to offer the behavior readily by showing the target to get her started and then making the target disappear.

8. Add distractions and be sure to go back to helping your dog with the target stick if the behavior falls apart.

Regardless of your dog's skill level, anyone can have fun teaching these simple tricks. Remember, the bottom line is to make sure you have

Boston Terrier targeting a target stick

fun while spending time with your best friend. Whether you teach your dog tricks to entertain your friends and family or you do therapy work in hospitals and nursing homes, having a dog that can do tricks shows off all her amazing attributes. Spending time together learning something new will enhance your bond and strengthen your relationship, making the quality of life better for both of you. I hope you enjoy teaching these tricks and I hope it inspires you to move on to the more complicated ones in the following chapters.

Social Graces

So your dog will shake hands and bow—that's something! Well, you can certainly expand his social skills to include a few kisses and pleasant conversation. The joy of having a dog is your interaction with each other. These next two behaviors really make the most of that.

Kiss Me

Teaching this behavior utilizes a combination of free shaping and luring. You are catching the dog in the act of doing the behavior and rewarding it, but you are getting the behavior started by prompting it first. The shaping steps for teaching Kiss Me are:

1. Using food to initially excite your dog is the key. Feed him a few small pieces of a treat and eat a few yourself, then stick your chin out and wait.
2. At the first sign of any attempt to open his mouth to lick you, click and treat.
3. Try putting the treats in your mouth and showing him they're there. Click and treat any attempt to lick you.
4. Add the verbal cue Kiss right before you think he's going to offer the behavior. Click and treat as the behavior happens.
5. Fade the food by showing it to the dog and putting it away on a counter or table and commanding Kiss. When he kisses, click and treat and run and get the treat.
6. Repeat this until the dog is beginning to offer the kiss as soon as you stick out your chin.

 ESSENTIALS Experimenting with different types of rewards will make you a more versatile and successful dog trainer. Experiment with food rewards, games, toys, and social opportunities (like letting your dog say hello to a person after your dog performs Sit). Know where and when to use these to improve your dog's training program.

Speak

Luring and free shaping, or a combination of the two, are the best tools for teaching this trick. The trick itself requires your dog to bark on cue.

1. Find something that causes your dog to bark, like a knock on the door or holding a treat out of range. Click and treat her when she barks.
2. Repeat at least twenty to twenty-five times.
3. Fake the antecedent to barking (the knock), and if your dog starts to bark, click and treat.
4. Verbally label the behavior Speak just before your dog barks.
5. Don't click and treat for any barking other than the one you ask for.
6. If she barks at inappropriate times, be obvious about turning your upper body away to let her know that extraneous barking will not be rewarded.

After basic obedience training skills (Sit, Stay, and Come), these simple tricks are the best opportunity for you and your dog to build a trusting and cooperative relationship. You'll develop a better understanding of how your dog thinks, and what motivates her, and your dog will learn to read your cues. Take the time to train your dog well—you'll both get the best results that way.

CHAPTER 7
Retrieving Tricks

Any dog can learn to pick something up in its mouth and bring it to his handler. Although some dogs have an instinctive talent to perform this behavior, even the most reluctant dog can learn to retrieve using operant conditioning by means of a clicker and treats.

Shaping the Retrieve

To shape the process of retrieving, break it down into tiny increments. Even dogs that are retrieving fanatics may refuse to pick up certain objects like keys or tools. Teaching a shaped retrieve using operant conditioning will not only make your dog a reliable retriever, it will also give you a strong base for teaching the retrieving tricks that follow.

When shaping a dog to retrieve it is best to pick an easy object to start with, something the dog is likely to pick up on his own. If you're not sure what texture appeals to your dog, set out a bunch of objects and see which he chooses to play with on his own. Most dogs don't like to pick up metal and have difficulty picking up small objects that require them to smoosh their nose into the floor trying to get their mouth around it. Choose something your dog can get his mouth around easily, such as a face cloth, a retrieving dumbbell, or a small empty box.

ESSENTIALS

When you are training for retrieving exercises, use an object that you can put away when the session is over. Keep the item "special," so that your dog looks forward to working with it every time you practice.

Using a novel object will make it more likely that your dog will at least investigate it, giving you a starting point for shaping the retrieve. Teach the retrieve by breaking it down into the most basic steps so that it will be resistant to falling apart later. The shaping steps to teach the retrieve are as follows:

1. Put an item on the floor about three feet away from your dog.
2. Click and treat him for moving toward it.
3. Click and treat him for touching the object with his nose.
4. Repeat this step about a dozen times and then withhold the click.
5. If he mouths the object at all, click and treat.
6. Once your dog is mouthing the object, withhold the click until he picks up the object.

7. Delay the click once more and build the time he will hold the object.
8. Add distance by putting the object a short distance away at first and gradually increasing it.
9. Label the retrieve Take It as the dog is picking up the object.
10. Label the release of the object Give or Leave It.

ALERT

Wait for your dog to get frustrated enough to actually close his mouth on the object before you click and treat. More than likely he will mouth the object quickly and release it, so be ready to click and give a jackpot.

Links and Chains

As tricks get more complicated, you realize that one command really represents several behaviors—a behavior chain. In training your dog to perform these more complicated tasks, you can use two approaches: the behavior chain or back chaining. Really, the only difference is whether you start with first things first or work your way backward from a successful conclusion.

Behavior Chains

The concept of a behavior chain is relatively simple. In order for your dog to bring his leash to you on the command Go Get Your Leash, he must: know where to find the leash; take it in his mouth (which may mean picking it up off the floor or pulling it from a doorknob); carry it to you in his mouth; and release it into your hand. Each of these steps is a link in the behavior chain, which is only as strong as its weakest element.

If your dog doesn't know how to carry objects without a lot of extra commands and prompting, behavior chain tricks will be choppy and uninteresting. Breaking things down into their component parts is a way of simplifying the trick and improving your dogs performance of it. A behavior chain is simply the breakdown of what the dog has to do in order to complete the behavior.

Back Chaining

Back chaining is related to behavior chains except instead of training step 1, step 2, step 3, you train it backwards, step 3, step 2, step 1. The idea is that if you train something backwards your dog will perform the behavior more reliably and with greater speed and enthusiasm because he is moving toward something he already knows well. By teaching him a multistep task backward, you are helping him remember the steps more easily because he learned the last one first. So in the case of the trick Bring Me Your Leash, it would be: hold the leash and release it into my hand; carry the leash to me from a distance; take it in your mouth; go find it.

SSENTIALS

If you come across an object that your dog refuses to retrieve, go back and reshape the retrieve using this object. If the retrieving part of the trick is weak because the dog is not comfortable retrieving this particular object, the performance of the trick will become sloppy and unreliable.

Each of these steps may need to be broken down further to meet your dogs individual needs, but the basic concept is the same. When the dog performs the whole trick, he will be moving from less familiar steps to more familiar steps. Because he learned the last part of the trick first, he will be more confident and flashy as he gets to the end and more reliable overall in his performance of the trick.

The Retrieving Tricks

Each of these tricks involves the dog retrieving or picking up something in its mouth and transferring it to another person. If your dog has any difficulty picking up the prop you are using, don't be afraid to go back to the basics steps of the retrieve using the new object. You will find that going back to kindergarten will help your dog's overall grasp of retrieving and will make him less likely to refuse to cooperate.

Go Get Your Leash

Lab Mix holding his leash

This trick involves having your dog retrieve his leash and bring it to you. To make this easier on the dog you may want to have one place that you leave your dog's leash, like on a doorknob or by the front door. The dog has to go to where the leash is kept and pull the leash off with his mouth. He needs to carry the leash to you and hold it until you take it from him.

If you teach this and the following behaviors using back chaining, you will find it easier for your dog to perform them because he is always moving toward the more familiar steps.

1. Hold the leash out and ask your dog to take it. Click and treat the exact moment he puts it in his mouth.
2. Back up a step and see if he will follow you; click and treat him for moving with the leash in his mouth.
3. Put the leash on the floor and tell him to Take It. As soon as he picks it up, click and treat.
4. Put the leash on the floor but don't click and treat until he takes it and takes several steps toward you.
5. Put the leash in various places at various distances and repeat. Click and treat for taking it under these new circumstances.
6. Gradually move the leash to where your dog can expect to find it and click and treat him for going to that spot.
7. Replace the Take It cue with Leash, by saying the new cue Leash right before the old cue. Gradually fade Take It so that your dog will perform the behavior on the new cue.

Get the Mail/Newspaper

This trick works well if you have a door slot for your mail or you have a daily newspaper that gets delivered to your door. For this trick, your dog has to go to where the mail or paper is kept, pick up the item, bring it to you, and release it into your hand.

1. Teach your dog to carry nonessential letters and junk mail without stopping to shred them before you use the real thing. ("The dog ate the mortgage bill" probably won't go over well with your spouse.) Do this by clicking and treating your dog for taking the letter or newspaper and holding it without mouthing it.
2. Take a step or two away and have her bring it to you. Click and treat the motion of moving toward you.
3. Put the letter on the floor and tell your dog to Take It. You may want to use junk mail for this part until your dog refines her techniques in picking up something so close to the floor.
4. When your dog is retrieving with finesse, begin to work her with the real mail pile or newspaper.
5. Label this behavior Mail or Paper by saying this new cue right before the current cue Take It; pretty soon your dog will be fetching with enthusiasm and finesse.

ESSENTIALS

Take retrieving on the road right away. Performing retrieving tricks in public is difficult; if you practice in different places from the start, your dog will be comfortable retrieving anywhere.

Go Find the Remote

Visitors, especially those with only a mild interest in dogs, love this trick—guests are always impressed when a dog can serve a useful purpose. If your housemate tends to hog the remote control, your dog can be your advocate in getting it back with a smile. For this trick, the dog has to find the remote, pick it up, carry it to you, and drop it in your hand.

1. Hand your dog the remote and click and treat him for holding it.
2. Back away a step or two and click and treat him for carrying it to you.
3. Put the remote on the couch or coffee table and tell your dog to Take It. Click and treat him for picking it up in his mouth.
4. Send him into the living room at greater distances and click and treat him when he finds the remote.
5. Call him to you as he gets the hang of this and click and treat him for holding it until you reach out to take it.
6. Replace Take It with the command Remote by offering the new cue right before the old cue "Take It."

Go Get the Phone

Nothing is better than having your own personal answering service. For this trick your dog has to go and retrieve the phone and bring it back to you. You may want to use a cordless phone for this (unless you sit close by) and store it on a low table or the floor to make it easy for your dog to reach it.

1. Hand your dog the receiver and tell her to Take It. Click and treat your dog for taking it in her mouth and holding it for a few seconds.
2. Hand your dog the phone and back away from her, encouraging her to follow you. Click and treat her for carrying the phone to you. Make sure the click happens while she is moving toward you, not when she arrives.
3. Repeat this step again, but now click and treat your dog for delivering the phone to you.
4. Put the phone on the floor and ask her to Take It; click and treat her for picking up the phone.
5. Put the phone at greater distances and have her retrieve it from further away. Time the click and treat for when your dog puts her mouth on the phone.
6. Increase the difficulty by delaying the click until she has the phone and is turning back to you. You can use a voice prompt like her name or the Come command.

7. Label the behavior Get the Phone by saying it right before the commands Take It and Come, until you can gradually fade the old commands and replace them with the new command Go Get the Phone.

8. Practice in short sessions until your dog begins to move toward the phone on the command Go Get the Phone.

Using a cordless phone for this trick is ideal, however you may want to start practicing with the receiver from an old phone to prevent damage to your existing one. Once the dog is pretty good at picking up the receiver without damaging it, make sure you make the real thing easily accessible to prevent dropping it or knocking it off the table.

Go Get Your Dish

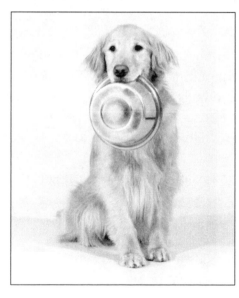

Golden Retriever holding his dinner bowl

This trick is a great way to show off your dog's intelligence. You'll probably want to keep his food dish in one spot so that he knows where to go to get it. For this trick your dog goes and brings his empty dish to you. Some dogs find it hard to retrieve metal dishes, in which case you may want to use a plastic one instead. If you decide to use the metal dish, don't be afraid to review the retrieving steps with this new object. The shaping steps are as follows:

1. Hand your dog his dish and tell him to Take It. Click and treat him for holding the dish.

2. Take a step away and call him to you. Click and treat him for moving toward you with the dish in his mouth.

3. Put the dish on the floor and tell him to Take It; click and treat him for picking up the dish.
4. Now, repeat this step but back away and click and treat the dog for picking up the dish and moving toward you.
5. Put the dish closer and closer to where you normally keep it and send him to take it over greater distances.
6. As your dog gets good at this replace Take It with the new verbal cue Wanna Eat? by saying the new cue right before the old cue, until the dog starts the behavior on the new cue.

FACTS

Some dogs hate having anything metal in their mouths. For these dogs you may want to go back to kindergarten and re-teach a retrieve with a metal object. See the shaping steps for teaching the retrieve and substitute the object with the metal bowl.

Find My Car Keys Please

If you are a person who constantly loses her keys this trick may save you a lot of time. For this trick your dog has to locate your keys by using her eyes and sense of smell, pick them up, bring them to you, and release them to your outstretched hand. The shaping steps are as follows:

1. Hand your dog your keys and tell her to Take It. Click and treat her for holding your keys.
2. Take a few steps back and call her to you. Click and treat her for moving toward you with the keys in her mouth.
3. Put the keys on the floor and tell her to Take It; click and treat her for picking up the keys.
4. Repeat the previous step but back away, and click and treat her for picking up the keys and moving toward you.
5. Put the keys in different places at varying distances and click and treat your dog for finding them. Vary where you put them, sometimes leaving them out in the open, sometimes leaving them concealed.
6. Gradually work it so that your dog is actively searching for your keys. When you are at this point, go ahead and label it Keys. Replace Take

It by giving the new cue Keys right before the old cue. Then, gradually fade the old cue.

7. Practice this one frequently to keep your dog motivated about searching for your keys.

Delivery Tricks

The fundamental skill involved in retrieval tricks is the dog's ability to carry things in his mouth. The secondary skill is the dog's ability to carry things in his mouth from one place to another. Delivery tricks simply change the "from" and "to," which, as these next few tricks will show, can be fun *and* functional.

Put Away Your Toys

This trick will impress your more practical non-dog-owning friends. A dog that picks up his own toys beats the heck out of a spouse or child that can't find the laundry hamper or put his dirty dishes in the sink. For this trick the dog has to pick up one toy at a time and put it in his toy box or basket. The shaping steps are as follows:

1. Hand your dog a toy and tell him to Take It; when he has the toy in his mouth, click and treat him for holding it.
2. Put the toy box between your feet and encourage the dog to come to you; click and treat him for holding the toy over the top of the box.
3. Repeat the above step, but ask the dog to Leave It as he holds the toy over the box.
4. Put the toy on the floor and tell him to Take It; click and treat him for picking up the toy.
5. Repeat the above step with more than one toy on the floor at a time.
6. Replace the Take It and Leave It cues with the new cue Toys Away by saying the new cue right before the old cue. Gradually fade the old cue.

Bring This to Daddy

This trick is great for dogs looking for a job to do. Having your very own canine delivery service is a great way for your dog to earn his keep. For this trick your dog has to pick up an object—a note, a tool, or any item reasonable for her to carry—and take it to someone else in the house. The shaping steps are as follows:

1. Hand your dog an object, using the command Take It, and have the helper call her from a step or two away. Click and treat her for moving toward that person.
2. Gradually move the helper greater and greater distances and click and treat the dog for moving away from you and toward your helper.
3. Gradually fade out the helper calling the dog, having the person go out of sight.
4. Replace the Take It command with Bring This to Daddy, by saying the new cue right before you say Take It. Click and treat the dog for taking the object and moving in the direction of the helper. Gradually fade out the old cue.
5. Vary the objects you have the dog carry, and practice often. This is the type of trick that gets better the more you practice it.

ESSENTIALS

Being a good dog trainer involves good planning. Trainers who plan ahead and map out their training sessions tend to have more success than those that don't. Clear goals and clear steps for reaching them are essential to knowing when your dog has arrived!

Mail a Letter

Teaching your dog to mail a letter is a fun and functional trick that uses lots of energy and is pretty entertaining to watch. Your dog must take a letter in his mouth, jump on the mailbox, and push the letter through the slot. He will need you to pull down the lever for him so he can drop the mail in the right spot. This trick is probably best taught to dogs tall enough to reach the top of the mailbox, unless you give your little one a boost. The shaping steps for teaching this trick are as follows:

1. Using the Touch command ask your dog to use his nose to push the letter into the slot. Click and treat him for touching his nose to the letter.
2. Withhold the click and treat until he pushes the letter a little further toward the slot this time.
3. Have him put two front paws on the mailbox and click and treat him for staying up for gradually longer periods of time. If you have a small dog, you may want to hold him close to the box and click him for putting his feet on the top.
4. Hand your dog a letter and tell him to Take It. Click and treat him for taking the letter, then for holding the letter for longer periods of time.
5. Call him to put his paws on the box while holding the letter, and click and treat.
6. Work on this step until the dog is easily balancing on his hind legs while holding the letter.
7. Now try to get the dog to leave the letter on the tray by telling him to Leave It and clicking and treating him for letting the letter go. You may need to adapt this trick for small dogs by holding them close to the box.
8. Practice all the steps until the whole thing is fluid and the dog responds to your command Take It by following through with all the other steps.
9. Replace the cue Take It with the new cue Mail It by saying the new cue right before the old cue and gradually fading the old cue.

Throw This in the Trash

Teach your dog to pick up anything you point to, including soda cans or other household items. This retrieving trick requires your dog to pick up the trash and release the object into a trash bin. To make it easier for your dog to get the trash into the container, you will probably want to use an open or swing-top trash bucket that is no taller than your dog's elbows.

1. Work with your dog and have her retrieve lots of different kinds of trash items, and have her bring them to you over increasingly longer distances.

2. Sit on a chair with the trash bucket between your feet. Tell your dog to pick up an item using the Take It cue, and call her to you; click and treat her when she is as close to the opening of the bucket as she'll come.

3. Repeat this step but delay the click by a few seconds until she is eventually standing with her chin right over the edge of the barrel.

4. With your dog standing close to the barrel, tell her to Leave It and click and treat her for releasing the trash. You will need to practice this so that your dog will eventually release the item right into the trash bucket.

5. Experiment by withholding the click until your dog makes a deliberate effort to drop the item in the barrel.

6. Label the behavior Throw It Away by saying this new cue right before the old cues Take It and Leave It. You will have to practice this many times before the new cue initiates the behavior.

7. Practice with different items so that your dog will retrieve and discard just about anything you ask her to.

FACTS

Consider the height of the trash basket and its opening when you are teaching this trick. The height of the basket needs to be proportionate to the dog's head so the opening is easily accessible. As you add distance to this trick you may want to even weight the basket so that it doesn't tip and scare the dog.

The Next Level

Just when you think you've covered pretty much everything, new games and tricks come along to keep you and your pet always learning together. Play them in your backyard, at the beach, or in the living room. Your dog is part of your family; if he's well trained, and well behaved, he'll be treated as such.

Let's Play Ring Toss

This old-fashioned game is a wonderful way to occupy a high-energy dog. For this trick the dog has to pick up each ring and place it on the post one at a time. This behavior is repeated until all three rings are on the post. You can buy a ring toss game inexpensively in any toy or department store. The shaping steps for this trick are as follows:

1. Hand your dog a ring and click and treat him for holding it.
2. Put the pole close to you and have the dog deliver the ring close to the post; click and treat him for releasing it over the post.
3. You may help the dog by tapping the post and encouraging him to drop it. Click and treat him for gradually closer attempts to leave the ring close to the post.
4. Withhold the click and treat and only click attempts to put the ring on the post.

With patience and time this can be a very entertaining game for your dog to play.

Sea Hunt

For this trick your dog has to fetch things out of a body of water. You can use a baby pool, the bathtub, a bucket, or a lake or pond. The goal for the dog is to retrieve all the items you sink or float and bring them back to dry land. This is a terrific warm-weather game because it gives your dog a great way to cool off. Fill up a baby pool with a few inches of water, depending on your dog's size, and sink some treasures for her to retrieve. The shaping steps for teaching your dog to play Sea Hunt are as follows:

1. Hold the object on the surface and ask the dog to Take It. Click and treat her for putting her mouth around it.
2. Hold the item just below the surface and click and treat the dog for dipping her nose under and taking it.

3. Gradually hold the item deeper until the dog is snagging it off the bottom.
4. Vary what you have the dog retrieve and keep the game light and fun.
5. Vary the depth of the water as your dog gets better at this game to make it more interesting and fun for everyone involved.

QUESTIONS?

Can I throw the object I want the dog to retrieve?
The object of these exercises is to train your dog to retrieve specific, stationary objects. Throwing objects, as you would in fetch, puts your dog into prey drive, a highly charged emotional state. It is best to leave the object stationary and let him figure out by your clicking which behaviors are rewardable and which are not.

Achoo! Can I Have a Tissue?

This trick is a real crowd pleaser. To perform this trick the dog has to retrieve a tissue on a sneeze cue. Who wouldn't be amazed by a dog getting you a tissue when you sneeze? For this trick you need a pop-up box of tissues and a convincing fake sneeze. The shaping steps for teaching this trick are as follows:

1. Hand the dog a tissue and click and treat him for taking it and holding it.
2. Take a step away and have him bring it to you. Click and treat him for moving toward you with the tissue in his mouth
3. Introduce the tissue box by pulling a tissue out and laying it across the top of the box. Click and treat him for taking the tissue off the top of the box.
4. Gradually tuck the tissue in so that the dog has to pull the tissue out to get his click and treat.
5. Replace the old cue Take It with the new cue Achoo! by saying the new cue right before the old cue. Click and treat the dog for starting the behavior as you sneeze.

Retrieving tricks are some of the most impressive because they involve several steps and highlight a dog's ability to think things through to put together a great performance. Each trick involves different props, but they all involve the same basic skill of being able to pick something up and carry it back to you. Reviewing the basic retrieve with the new item is a great way to warm up any new trick regardless of how experienced your dog is.

ESSENTIALS

Teach your dog to grab a tissue without tearing it in a million pieces by giving her lots of opportunities to practice, and by not letting her hold the tissue for too long. You may also want to keep the tissue box in one place so the dog knows where to go to get a tissue when you sneeze.

CHAPTER 8
Show-Off Tricks

We all have a little show-off in us, and dogs are no exception. Dogs love to make us laugh and their antics often cheer us and relieve the stresses of everyday life. Taking the time to work with your dog will strengthen your bond with her and fine-tune your ability to communicate with each other. Your dog will love strutting her stuff.

Fancy Dogs

Some dogs, because of their breeds or their personalities, just seem to be suited to elegant tricks. That's why it's so important to know your dog and understand him—so you can train him to his best advantage.

Show Me Your Best Side

When your dog is performing this trick, she looks as though she is posing for a picture. This trick requires your dog to turn her head to the side and hold it. The easiest way to teach this trick is by free shaping, which means limiting the dog's options and catching the right behaviors with a click and treat to shape the dog into the actual position that you are looking for.

1. Start with your dog facing you in a Sit and click and treat her for staying.
2. After about thirty seconds or so, stop clicking and watch her closely; if she turns her head at all, click and treat.
3. Pick one side or the other to start with and click any head turns in that direction.
4. When your dog starts to understand that turning her head is causing the click, it's time to delay the click by a few seconds to encourage her to hold the position.
5. Gradually increase the seconds by a few at a time until your dog will turn her head to the side and hold it for fifteen seconds.
6. Label the behavior Pose just before she offers the turn of her head. Repeat until the command Pose causes the behavior.

Push a Baby Carriage

This trick is adorable, but for safety's sake it should not be practiced with a real baby. A doll carriage with a baby doll is safer. This trick requires the dog to stand and walk on his hind legs while pushing the carriage with his front feet. The shaping steps for teaching Push a Baby Carriage are as follows.

1. Start out by getting your dog to sniff the baby carriage, and click and treat.
2. Secure the carriage so that it won't roll, and use a target to get your dog to put his front paws on the handle; click and treat.
3. Get your dog to hold the position by delaying the click and treat by a second or two.
4. Fix the carriage so that it will roll only a short distance (use blocks of wood behind the wheels), and click and treat your dog for moving the carriage a little at a time.
5. Encourage your dog to move the carriage and click and treat him for complying.
6. Control how far the carriage rolls to avoid scaring your dog.
7. You can label this behavior Push by saying this cue as the dog is moving the carriage.

ESSENTIALS

To prevent the carriage from tipping, weight the seat with some heavy books so that when your dog jumps up to touch the handle the carriage stays stable and stationary. Be sure the wheels are locked or use wood blocks to prevent the carriage from rolling away too soon.

Hi-Ho Silver, Away!

This trick, inspired by a horse-loving friend of mine, is a great way to show off a dog that likes to jump up on you. The only difference is your dog is not making physical contact with you when she is holding the rearing-horse position with her front legs stretched upward. The shaping steps for teaching Hi-Ho Silver, Away! are as follows:

1. Hold your hand as a target above your dog's head and click and treat her for touching it.
2. Gradually raise your hand until she is all the way up on her hind legs.
3. Practice frequently to help her build up her leg muscles.

4. Get your dog to hold the position by delaying the click and treat for several seconds.
5. Increase the time by a few seconds until she can hold the position for about fifteen seconds.
6. Cue your dog to extend her paws by using the Paw It command with your hand as a target.
7. Only click and treat versions of this behavior that are of longer duration and the right position (front paws extended).
8. Fade the hand target by using it to start the behavior and then pulling it away. Click and treat your dog for continuing to perform the behavior in the absence of the target.
9. Replace the old cue with the new cue Away by saying the new cue right before the dog starts the behavior.

Sit Up Pretty

For this trick the dog is sitting on his hind legs with his front paws tucked into his chest. This is also a behavior that the dog needs to practice frequently to be able to build up his back and hind-end muscles. The shaping steps for teaching Sit Up Pretty are as follows:

1. Use your hand as a target and click and treat him for touching your hand while raising his front end off the ground.
2. Withhold the click and treat by a few seconds to get your dog to hold the position high enough to have him sitting up on his back end, but not standing.
3. Add a cue like Sit Up or Beg, by saying it right before the Touch cue.
4. The click and treat should happen as soon as the dog starts the behavior on the new cue.

ESSENTIALS

Practice fading your hand as a target by presenting it but clicking before your dog actually touches it. By clicking your dog early so that she is on her way to touching your hand but doesn't actually make contact with it, she will be less dependent on its presence and it will be easier to fade.

Balance a Cookie on Your Nose

This trick demonstrates your dog's will power, because she must balance a cookie on her nose and wait to take the cookie until you say so.

1. Start with your dog in a Sit in front of you and click and treat her for staying.
2. Practice holding her muzzle and placing a cookie on her nose for a click and treat.
3. Repeat this last step until the dog can hold still for several seconds.
4. Slowly let go of your dog's muzzle and click and treat her for holding it steady.
5. Gradually increase the amount of time your dog balances the cookie on her nose before you click and treat.
6. You will probably find after a bit of practice that your dog develops a flip-and-catch technique to eat the cookie. This makes the trick all the more flashy and impressive.

Humble Dogs

Although some dogs are prone to fancier tricks, others are, by nature, more sedate. These simple and adorable tricks suit their personalities, and will therefore be easier for you to teach. How you use the tricks, such as Say You're Sorry, is entirely up to you.

Say You're Sorry

For this trick the dog lies down with his chin on the ground between his front paws. An added bonus is teaching him to look up at you, which will add an even more convincing element to the performance. You may want to use this as the canine version of Time Out.

1. Put your dog in a Down, facing you; click and treat him for holding that position.
2. After about thirty seconds, withhold the click and wait. Pay close attention and click and treat any head motion down.

German Shepherd saying he's "sorry"

3. Once your dog starts to understand that lowering his head is what causes the click, withhold the click until your dog holds the position for an extra second.
4. Increase the number of seconds your dog has to keep his head down until you can build it up to fifteen to twenty seconds.
5. Label the behavior Sorry by saying the command right before he offers the behavior.
6. Repeat this step until the command Sorry triggers the behavior.

ESSENTIALS

To help your dog understand that lowering his head is what is causing the click, deliver the treat low to encourage the dog to look down. This will give you more opportunities to reward him for offering the right behavior.

Say Your Prayers

Whether they are praying for leniency after getting into the garbage or praying for mud to roll in, any dog looks cute performing this trick. This trick requires your dog to rest her paws on a chair or stool and tuck her head between her front paws. She can be sitting or standing when she does this.

1. Use a table, stool, or chair that won't move when your dog puts her paws on it.
2. Get your dog to put her front paws on the stool by tapping the stool or luring her with a treat. Click any effort to get her paws up on the stool.
3. Delay the click so that your dog is putting her paws up and leaving them there for three seconds before you click and treat.
4. Using a yogurt lid as a target, get your dog to put her head between her front paws by placing the target slightly under her chest. Click and treat your dog for making attempts to touch the target.
5. Delay the click again until your dog holds her nose to the target for longer periods of time.
6. Fade the target slowly by clicking before she actually touches it, or by making it smaller.
7. Label the behavior Say Your Prayers as she is performing the behavior and just before any other cues. Gradually fade any old cues.

ESSENTIALS

To make the trick Say Your Prayers go more smoothly and to prevent your dog from scaring himself, you'll want to choose a low stool that he can put his paws up on easily but that won't slide across the floor when he leans on it. Consider doing this trick on a rug or putting nonskid material under the legs of the stool.

Family Tricks

As your dog's handler, you are her connection to the human world. If your dog is part of a larger family, however, each member of the family needs to have a good working relationship with your dog. Start training your dog as an active participant in family life—everyone will benefit from it.

Go Wake Up Daddy

What better way to wake up each morning than with a canine alarm clock? This trick requires a kiss or a nudge to the person the dog is waking up. You'll need a helper to act as the person the dog is supposed to rouse.

1. Start with the helper lying face down with his head on his folded arms. Have your helper hide a handful of lures under his arm and encourage your dog to investigate. When your dog goes to stick her nose under the helper's arm, click and treat.
2. Fade the lures in the helper's hand until the dog is nudging the person without the food being present. Click and treat any attempt to burrow under the person's arm.
3. Label the behavior Wake Up and the person's name just before the dog burrows under the person's arm.
4. Send your dog from gradually increasing distances until she is eagerly performing Wake Up from a room or two away.
5. Change helpers so that each member of the family gets a turn to be awakened by the dog.
6. Practice every Saturday morning to make sure no one misses out on breakfast!

ESSENTIALS

As your dog begins to understand the concept of going and waking someone up, you can start to teach her to wake up specific people by having the person call her after you give the Wake Up command. You can wean your dog off this later when she begins to catch on.

Go Get Mom

This is a useful trick for kids and parents alike; for this trick the dog must go to a family member and lead them back to the person that sent them. What better way to round up the family for dinnertime then to send the dog to bring each member to the table.

1. Using the person your dog is going to get as your helper, call the dog back and forth between you and click and treat him for going to each person.
2. When your dog is doing this enthusiastically, label the behavior Go and the person's name right before the person calls the dog to Come.
3. Gradually move the people further apart so that the dog is going to the person from different rooms and up and down the stairs.
4. Replace the Come command with Go by saying Go Get Mom right before Mom calls the dog to come. The person the dog is searching for should be doing the clicking and treating when the dog finds them.
5. Once the dog starts to offer the behavior readily, he can be weaned off the clicker and treats, but he should still be acknowledged with praise and affection.

Supersmart Tricks

You learned earlier that dogs can be trained to perform any task that they are physically capable of doing. That said, the critical factor to successfully performing these tricks is your patience in handling your dog. Using your tools (see Chapter 4), and chain methods (see Chapter 7), start training your dog for these actions when you see that she is ready.

Ring a Bell

This trick involves teaching your dog to ring a bell with her nose or a paw. This trick is also quite practical, as you can teach your dog to ring a bell when she wants to go outside to the bathroom.

Hang a set of bells next to the door that you normally use to let your dog outside. Once she learns how to ring the bell with her mouth or nose, start having her do this each time she goes out to go potty. Pretty soon your dog will ring the bell to let you know she wants to go out. You may want to use a set of sleigh bells for this trick; four or five bells on a long strap may make it easier for your dog to learn to ring a bell, because it will give her more opportunities to be right.

The shaping steps for teaching your dog to Ring a Bell are as follows:

1. Put the bells on the floor and click and treat your dog for sniffing them (you can use a Touch command if she knows one).
2. Delay the click and wait for her to touch harder or mouth them before you click and treat.
3. Work at this until she's ringing the bells with purpose.
4. Hang the bells next to the door and repeat the above steps until she is ringing them reliably.
5. Gradually increase the distance she must travel to touch the bells.
6. Verbally label ringing the bells, Bells.

Dancing Dog

This trick is adorable but difficult for most dogs. To perform this trick the dog must balance on his hind legs and walk. You'll want to practice in short sessions to help your dog build up his back and leg muscles gradually. Be sure to work on a nonskid surface so that your dog does not injure himself. The shaping steps for teaching Dancing Dog are as follows:

1. With your dog in a Sit, hold your hand slightly above his nose and click and treat any effort to raise himself up on his back legs to touch your hand.
2. Raise your hand higher and continue to click and treat your dog for using his hind end to raise himself up and touch your hand.
3. Get your dog to hold the position longer by delaying the click by a second or two.
4. Gradually increase the time to several seconds.
5. Move your hand around and click and treat him for walking on his hind legs to touch it.
6. Turn your hand in a circle and click and treat your dog for walking on his hind legs to follow it.
7. Add the cue Dance by saying it just before the dog starts the behavior.

Get Me a Bottle of Water

This amazing trick involves your dog opening the refrigerator, taking out a bottle of water, closing the door, and bringing the bottle of water to you. You'll probably want to start with a water bottle and then as your dog refines her techniques, you can change the water bottle to a can of soda or a bottle of juice. This trick has three different parts: retrieving the bottle, opening the refrigerator door, and closing the refrigerator door.

Getting the Water Bottle

1. Hand your dog a bottle of water and tell her to Take It. Click and treat your dog for hanging on to it for several seconds at a time.
2. Move away from your dog and have her come to you over greater and greater distances. Click and treat her first as she is moving to you, and then for delivering the bottle to your hand.
3. Place the bottle on the floor and tell your dog to Take It, then Bring It. Click and treat her for retrieving it, then gradually withhold the click until the dog is on her way back to you.
4. Put the bottle on a low shelf of the refrigerator and practice having the dog Take It. Click and treat your dog for at first approaching, then taking, then bringing the bottle to you over short training sessions.

Golden Retriever with her baby bottle

Opening the Refrigerator Door

1. Put a strap on the refrigerator door to make it easier for you dog to open it.
2. Starting with the refrigerator door open, hand your dog the strap and tell him Take It. Click and treat him for taking the strap.
3. Once your dog is taking the strap easily, delay the click for an extra second or two and click and treat your dog for holding it.
4. Standing slightly behind your dog, call him back to you while he holds the strap. You may need to go back and teach your dog the formal retrieve (see Chapter 7) with the strap or at least review it with him.
5. When he can hold onto the strap while backing up, click and treat him for actually moving the door.
6. Gradually close the door until it's almost clicked shut, so that your dog has to pull harder to open it.
7. Once your dog can open it when it's shut all the way, try letting him retrieve the strap on his own. At first, click and treat any attempt to take the strap.
8. Gradually add a little distance so that your dog is approaching the refrigerator from greater and greater distances.
9. Eventually delay your click so that your dog is taking the strap and starting to back up to pull the door open before you click. If at any time he seems confused and the behavior falls apart, go back and break things down into smaller parts and gradually rebuild the behavior.

Close the Door (dog uses his nose)

1. Once your dog is comfortable holding the bottle in his mouth, practice having him target the refrigerator door with his nose.
2. Open the door a little, give a Touch command, and click and treat him for moving the door shut even a little.
3. Gradually leave the door open a little more until the dog is shutting the door with purpose. Make sure you click and treat your dog for even small attempts to push the door shut.
4. Verbally label the behavior Shut the Door.

Close the Door (dog uses his paws)

An alternate option would be to have your dog use his paws on the refrigerator to close it (see Chapter 4).

1. Use a paw target to get him to touch the refrigerator with his paws, then click and treat.
2. Open the door a little and tell your dog to paw the door; click and treat him for moving the door shut.
3. Gradually open the door more so your dog has to push the door harder to earn the click and treat.
4. Verbally label the behavior Shut the Door.

Be careful what item you choose for your dog to retrieve. Water bottles are the easiest for the dog to grasp at first, and later you can work up to retrieving cans or glass. If you have a dog that tends to bite down hard when he retrieves things, you may want to practice with empty cans first to prevent him from scaring himself or making a mess of your kitchen.

Review each piece to put them all together. Open the refrigerator door (keep the bottle on the lower shelf), and have your dog take the bottle. When he still has the bottle in his mouth, call him around the door and tell him to push it shut. Practice these two steps until they are fluid. Then add the command to Take It (the door strap), followed by retrieving the bottle. Practice these together until they are fluid. Then, combine them with closing the door. You may have to go back and forth a bit in order to keep each part of the behavior strong until eventually it is one continuous behavior.

Go Left, Go Right

Teaching your dog how to distinguish from his left and right will amaze your friends and family. It will also enable you to direct your dog to exactly where you want her to go.

1. Start with your dog in front of an object (like a chair or a hassock) and put a target lid to the left of it about three feet away.
2. Send your dog to go Touch, and click and treat her for responding.
3. Repeat this at gradually increasing distances, clicking right before your dog touches her nose to the target.
4. When your dog is offering the behavior readily, say the new cue Go Left just before she is about to move forward to touch the target. Repeat this until she will go to the left when you say left.
5. Fade the target by making it smaller (use scissors to cut it into smaller pieces) until your dog simply moves left on command.
6. To teach your dog to go right, simply follow all the same steps except with everything on the right.

You can combine the Go Left and Go Right commands with retrieving tricks by lining up several objects in a row and asking your dog to take the one on the left or the right. If nothing else, this trick will give you a better foundation for teaching your dog more complicated tricks.

Find It

Sending your dog to find something you have lost is useful and exciting to the dog. Losing your wallet or keys in a pile of leaves or along your walking route could be disastrous—unless your dog can help in the search.

1. Choose an item with lots of your scent on it (like a hat or a hair tie) and show it to your dog.
2. Have someone hold your dog's collar while you hide the item somewhere obvious at first.
3. Release your dog to go find it and click and treat him as he approaches it.
4. Gradually increase the difficulty by hiding it in more challenging places.
5. Find another item to practice with and try again.
6. Label the behavior Find It as the dog moves toward the object.

Multi-Dog Tricks

Successful multi-dog tricks require that each dog understands the behavior and can perform it on a reliable cue. Before attempting it with more than one dog, go over the steps with each dog individually. If things fall apart or don't go as well as planned, review the steps with each dog separately.

ESSENTIALS

These tricks are meant to be performed by two or three dogs at once. You may want to enlist the help of multiple handlers, one for each dog. The helpers' roles will be to reinforce and reward individual dogs for performing correctly while they get used to performing tricks as a team.

Double-Dog Roll Over

This trick involves two dogs rolling over at the same time. As you position the dogs, make sure that you leave enough space in between them so that they don't crash into each other. Another way you could perform this trick would be to have the dogs roll over one at a time, one right after the other. Shaping steps for the Double-Dog Roll Over are as follows:

1. Have each dog lie about three feet apart (allow more space if the dogs are giant breeds).
2. Reinforce each dog for holding the Down/Stay position.
3. Cue the dogs to Roll Over one at a time (reinforce the others for staying until they have been cued), or give the cue for all the dogs to roll at the same time.
4. Experiment with giving a cue to each dog and then giving one cue to the group and see which version of the trick looks flashier.
5. If you are cueing all the dogs at once, you need only one click for all of them, but treat each dog with her own cookie.
6. If you are cueing each dog separately, click and treat that dog before asking the next one to go.

7. Once the dogs are performing reliably, go ahead and verbally label the behavior Everybody Over, or label each individual rollover with the dog's name and then the Roll Over command.

Pass the Cookie Please

This trick requires two dogs, one sitting in front of the other. The first dog balances a cookie on his nose and on cue, tosses his head back, flinging the cookie over his head to the dog sitting behind him. The dog sitting behind him catches it and eats it as his reward.

Shaping steps for teaching the first dog to balance a cookie on his nose are as follows:

1. Choose a flat cookie to help the dog learn to balance it.
2. Hold your dog's muzzle still and click and treat him for allowing you to do this.
3. Place a dog biscuit on the flat part of the top of his muzzle and click and treat him for holding his head still.
4. Use a Stay command and frequent clicks and treats to help your dog learn to balance the cookie on his nose.
5. Once he's got the balancing part, you can click after a certain number of seconds and release him to flip the cookie off his nose.

FACTS

It requires good timing of the click to get your dog to understand that it's the toss of his head that you are looking for. Most dogs will toss their heads back to get the cookie off their nose. Some will even flip it and catch it if you practice enough. It's important that you let your dog develop his own style by practicing frequently.

Add the second dog to the mix once your cookie-balancing dog has a good toss and is no longer immediately pursuing the dropped cookie. Practice having the second dog catch the cookie after the first dog tosses it. This may require lots of practice to get the timing and coordination just right. The commands or labels will be Hold It, Stay, and then Okay, which will cause the dog holding the cookie to toss the cookie, which will be caught by the dog behind him. Be sure you click and treat the first dog for not pursuing the tossed cookie.

ESSENTIALS
> When having a group of dogs perform together, you might like to stagger the behaviors so that the dogs perform them one after the other. Initially, you may want to use a helper to reinforce the dogs that are waiting for their turn.

Everybody Wave

This adorable trick can be performed with any amount of dogs. The dogs should line up facing their audience and raise a paw in the air as if waving hello. The shaping steps for teaching a group of dogs to wave are as follows:

1. Make sure each dog can fluently and reliably wave on a hand signal.
2. Line the dogs up and reinforce them for holding a Stay.
3. Cue the dogs to Wave and click and treat all of them.
4. Practice with two dogs at a time until they are competing with each other to raise their paws the fastest.
5. Encourage extra-fast efforts by clicking and treating only the dog that was first.
6. Gradually add more dogs, following the same rules; the faster dogs get treated more often than the slower dogs.
7. If one dog is particularly slow, take him aside and teach him to wave faster before putting him back into the group.

This trick is an adorable way to say hello or good-bye during a visit with school children or a visit at a nursing home. You can vary how you have the dogs perform it by having them wave individually or as a group. You can also improve on each dog's individual wave by only clicking and treating the best versions of the wave, one aspect at a time. For instance, you might improve the speed of the dog's response by giving the cue and only clicking and treating when he offers the behavior within a certain amount of time (say three seconds). You might improve the height of the wave by only clicking and treating the higher waves and ignoring the lower ones, telling the dog to try again. Just be sure that you are concentrating on one aspect at a time so as not to confuse the dog.

Leap Frog

Be careful which dogs you choose for this trick; not all dogs are comfortable having other dogs jump over them. This trick requires two to three dogs. While the rest of the dogs lie down about three feet apart, the third dog leaps over their backs and lies down next to the last dog. The first dog then repeats this, and so on.

1. Reinforce all the dogs for lying down and holding the Stay.
2. Work the first dog by having her touch her nose to the target stick held over the back of the first dog. Use the target stick to help her hop over the other dogs one at a time; click and treat each hop.
3. When the last dog has been hopped over, have her lie down and let the next dog go.
4. Reinforce the other dogs for holding the Down/Stay position. You may need a helper for this.
5. To increase your dog's tolerance for being hopped over, practice reinforcing your dog for letting you step over her.
6. Adding speed to this trick will make it impressive and flashy; just be sure to build up to it slowly and don't rush the dogs. When they are comfortable they will move faster.

Evaluate the dogs that you use for this trick carefully and be sure that they don't mind having a dog jump over their back. This is not a trick that every dog will tolerate.

Take a Bow

For this trick the dog brings his front end close to the ground, with his chest resting on the floor, lifts his tail end in the air, and holds the position. You can have the dogs do it all at the same time or one after the other.

1. It's probably best to start with all the dogs in the Sit/Stay position. Reinforce each dog for holding the Stay.
2. Give the cue for Bow to all the dogs at once, or each dog individually. Click and treat those dogs that perform the behavior correctly.
3. Continue to practice until all the dogs are performing in unison. Don't be afraid to go back and review the steps with each dog individually if the trick starts to fall apart. (See Chapter 6 for the shaping steps for teaching your dog to bow.)

If you are going to train multiple dogs to work together, it's a good idea to make sure they get along well and are not competitive over food. Each dog should be taught how to perform the behavior separately until the trick is on a reliable cue before being asked to perform it in a group. If you do not have the behavior reliably on cue with the dogs individually, a group training session will be a frustrating experience for all of you.

Walking the Dog

This trick involves two dogs. One dog wears a collar and leash and the other dog carries the leash in her mouth.

1. Teach your dog to retrieve and carry a leash. (See Chapter 7 for shaping the retrieve behavior.)
2. Once your dog is retrieving the leash easily, start practicing having her hold it with some resistance (hold on to the end and give a little tug).
3. Hand your dog the leash and click and treat her for grabbing it and walking with you.
4. With the leash firmly in your dog's mouth, practice giving it a tug, and click and treat her for pulling back or hanging on.
5. Gradually increase the amount of resistance you offer to prepare her for a real dog on the end of the lead.
6. When she can carry the leash while you are offering resistance, go ahead and add a real dog.

7. The dog you add should be an adult with some leash manners and the leash should be attached to a flat buckled collar.
8. The dog being led should be clicked and treated for walking slightly ahead of the other dog but not outright pulling.

Tips for a Better Performance

When working with multiple dogs it quickly becomes apparent that the better able the dogs are to perform the tricks alone, the more likely they are to cooperate as a group. There are some tricks to working with groups of dogs that understand what is expected but need to learn how to do the behavior in unison.

*   Only treat those dogs that perform the trick fast.
*   Point to the individual dog that you are working with as you give the cue.
*   Use a helper to reward the other dogs for holding a Stay while you work with an individual dog.
*   Review tricks regularly with each individual dog to keep performance consistent.
*   Vary the quality and quantity of treats to keep your dog guessing and trying harder to earn the next goodie.
*   Keep your sessions short and frequent to keep the dogs focused and sharp.

ESSENTIALS It can't be stressed enough that if you don't reward the dogs that are waiting their turn to perform, you will lose their interest. Rewarding the dogs that are waiting will ensure that all the dogs stay focused and ready to work.

The show-off in every dog is something to celebrate! Let your dog—or dogs—indulge her sense of humor and excitement by making her part of your entertainment committee. Enjoy spending time teaching your dog tricks and performing them for friends and family. Developing a healthy training relationship with your dog will make it easier to communicate with her and help you to gain control of behavior problems.

CHAPTER 9

Techniques and Tools for Problem Solving

I f you don't train your dog or provide any structure, you will be rewarded with a dog that behaves exactly as you taught him to behave: in ways that are out of control, demanding, mischievous, and destructive. Invest the time, patience, and love to get your dog off to a good start and you will have a companion that enhances the life of you and your family.

Set the Best Environment

Living with a dog need not be complicated, but with the changing demands of life in our world, dogs are left to cope with an amazing amount of stress and changes that their ancestors were never asked to

Welsh Terrier jumping through a hoop

deal with. To say that our full schedules are going to change dramatically when we take on a dog as a member of our family is unrealistic; however, we must make accommodations for them and be sure we meet their needs. If we are unable or unwilling to spend more time at home with our pets, we must be willing to hire someone to take care of their needs for us.

Dogs are pack animals that were meant to live in groups; they are not solitary animals and do not enjoy spending hours alone for days at a time. The root of many dogs' behavior problems lies in a lack of stimulation and energy outlets. Most people can't just quit their jobs to stay at home with the dog, but the emergence of quality doggie day care programs, reputable pet sitters, and dog parks has made it possible to own a dog and have a busy life.

QUESTIONS?

Who will exercise your dog if you can't?
For many dogs, having a dog walker to play with in the middle of the day, or spending a day at a doggie day care center, is not a frivolous luxury; it's necessary exercise and social time with other dogs and people.

Behavior problems in dogs lead many people to seek help from a dog trainer or attend a group training class. Problems usually range from jumping or mouthing, to excessive barking or aggression. If you visit an animal shelter you will see many dogs between the age of nine months and two years, whose families simply didn't have time for their energy and antics. Behavior problems don't have to lead to the dog being left at an animal shelter if you understand a little about how dogs think and what motivates them to do what they do.

When you take a dog into your home, you must make room for him. Dogs require a lot of love and training and care, but they give so much more back in loyalty and love. Be sure to give her the best home you possibly can—you will be rewarded a hundred fold. If your dog's behavior is less than ideal, don't give up on her. All dogs, no matter how sweet and compliant they are, need training, limits, exercise, and house rules.

Analyze the Problem

When it comes to trying to solve a dog's behavior problem, people often think too much. They blame the dog for going potty on the carpet out of spite when in reality the dog isn't being walked enough! Let's be clear, here: Dogs don't hold grudges, they don't do things out of spite, and they are not sorry for anything! Dogs are not capable of those thoughts. They live in the moment, they are opportunistic, and they repeat behavior that is rewarded, even if it's rewarded negatively. That's why we like dogs, remember? They are not little people in fur suits; they are dogs.

Dogs are animals, and animals do things that sometimes baffle humans, despite our best attempts to understand them. In order to solve an existing behavior problem, it is crucial to sit down with your family members and figure out the details of the problem. Using the following questions as a guide, try to identify and define what the dog is actually doing, when he is doing it, and what you might be able to teach him to do instead.

> **Identify the problem.** What does the dog actually do? Write it down and describe it in as much detail as possible.
>
> **Cause.** What triggers the dog to do the behavior? Is it the presence of a strange dog, the doorbell, or a new person?

Frequency. How often does the dog do the behavior? Once a minute, nonstop, every time the trigger is present, only half the time?

Consequence. What has been done to stop the behavior? What consequence results when the dog responds to the trigger?

Reinforcement history. How long has the dog been doing the behavior and what about it is reinforcing him to repeat it?

Management. What can you do to prevent the dog from practicing the behavior while you are retraining him?

By identifying the actual source of the problem, you will be able to develop a plan for retraining the dog to respond in a more appropriate way. Let everyone who takes care of the dog participate in the exercise, as well as future training sessions.

Behavior Management

Prevention isn't training, but it can help you get rid of unwanted behavior, because you are not allowing the dog to practice it repeatedly. "Management" involves putting the dog in a separate room or crate when visitors come or stepping on the leash to prevent the dog from jumping. The less the dog gets to practice the wrong behavior, the less you will have to do to convince him that the right behavior is more rewarding and desirable. Behavior management does *not* mean correcting, reprimanding, or punishing your dog.

Some people manage their dog's behavior with crates, gates, and pens; others use leashes or time outs. It doesn't matter how you manage your dog's behavior, as long as it keeps your dog from practicing the wrong behavior over and over. You want to change problem behavior, and management prevents the dog from rewarding himself. Consider these behavior management ideas:

- Use a crate when you can't watch your dog, if he is a destructive chewer.
- Keep a leash on your dog when company visits, and put your foot on it to prevent jumping.

- Don't allow your dog off leash in public places if he doesn't come when he's called.
- Avoid other dogs if your dog is aggressive around them.
- If your dog likes to escape out the front door, deny access to it.
- If your dog likes to bite the mailman, don't tie him outside the front door.
- If your dog is not fully housebroken, don't allow him unsupervised freedom.

Management and prevention are things you can do to keep a behavior problem from perpetuating itself; use them while you are retraining your dog to do something more appropriate. Prevention is not a 100 percent solution, but it can help you move toward your goal by not reinforcing any inappropriate behavior.

Alternate Behavior

Okay. You've gotten to the root of the bad behavior, and you have an interim plan in place—management. The next step is understanding reinforcement and replacement behavior. You need to provide reinforcement for a behavior other than the one you don't like. Otherwise, the dog will revert back to the old behavior. Think about reinforcing a behavior that is easy to teach and easy for the dog to perform, even with a lot of distractions.

ESSENTIALS
Most dog owners know exactly what they want their dogs to stop doing, but very few have put thought into what the dog should do instead. Unless you develop a plan for an acceptable alternate, you will not get rid of problem behavior.

What Reinforces the Wrong Behavior?

Look closely at the circumstances surrounding the misbehavior and see what the dog finds reinforcing about it. If he jumps and people yell at him and shove him off, perhaps he likes the attention and they should ignore him instead. Maybe there is a member of your household that encourages the dog to jump and isn't consistent about reinforcing the dog for sitting instead.

By removing the source of the reinforcement, you can put a good dent in getting rid of a behavior problem. In many cases the dog is getting way too much attention for the wrong behavior and needs more information about what is going right. If there isn't anything going right, then the dog has too much freedom and too many options. In this case, you'll need to rethink your training program and make it easier for your dog to be right.

Reinforcing the Right Behavior

To change a behavior that has become a habit, you need to provide a high rate of reinforcement for the appropriate behavior or it will never occur to the dog to try anything else. Dogs do what works, so if they get attention for the wrong behavior, they are likely to repeat it in the future. If they are reinforced for a more appropriate behavior with really yummy treats or exciting games of fetch, they will tend to make the good things happen again by repeating the behavior.

FACTS

Providing an undesirable consequence for a behavior, such as turning away from a barking dog, is very effective in changing the behavior. Being ignored was not the outcome the dog expected; by ignoring him you are saying that barking doesn't work.

Every reinforcement for the right behavior is like money in the bank. If your dog's bank account for the undesirable behavior is high, you will need to build up a considerable history of reinforcement of the alternate behavior. Practice often, give occasional jackpots (a handful of small goodies or an extra-long game of fetch or tug), and set your dog up to succeed.

Training an Incompatible Behavior

Teaching the dog an acceptable behavior solves many behavior problems because a dog can't necessarily do two things at once. For instance, a dog can't sit politely to greet a stranger and jump on them at the same time. Giving the dog an alternate behavior gives you more control over her, and it also allows you to reward her for an appropriate response. Perhaps your dog could:

- Greet visitors with a toy in her mouth instead of jumping on them.
- Go to her bed or mat when the doorbell rings.
- Do a play bow when she sees another dog.
- Retrieve a toy instead of barking at the window at passersby.
- Look at you instead of lunging at other dogs.
- Target your hand (see Chapter 4) instead of running away.

Use this opportunity to be creative, and find solutions that suit your needs and your dog's natural inclinations. Think of this as another way you're making it easy for training to be successful.

Problem-Solving Tools

Every dog owner needs to be armed with tools and tricks to teach their dog how to live with people in a safe, relaxed manner. Knowing your dog—his energy level, his tolerance of other dogs, his likes and dislikes—will be a huge asset in training him to respond to you in appropriate ways.

The most reliable outcome of punishment is a breakdown of the relationship and the trust that we have worked so hard to cultivate. Punishment doesn't change behavior permanently unless there is incentive to do something else.

Map out the changes to your dog's routine that you have decided to implement, and determine a time frame for training him. Set up a schedule of consistent practice times so that you teach each part of each behavior in small digestible portions, to be built upon each time you work your dog. Make sure you also consider the whole dog, mind and body, and provide for all of your dog's needs.

Exercise

Don't let this get by you. Playing, running, fetching, and having time with you is crucial to a dog's sanity. Be sure that your dog gets at least thirty to sixty minutes a day of all-out running or playtime with other dogs before you even consider training him to be a better companion. If your dog has tons of toys but only plays with a few, consider grouping them in sets of ten and rotating them each week to keep things interesting. Make a play date with your neighbor's dog, sign up for doggie day care, or hire a pet sitter to exercise your dog while you're at work so that when you come home you can concentrate on training your dog and have a willing student who is ready to work.

Basic Obedience

Nothing beats the companionship of a well-trained dog. A dog that responds to Sit, Down, and Come is a dog that can be taken many places and not put you to shame. Spend time teaching these basics, at first in an environment with only a few distractions and then build up to being able to work somewhere outdoors or around other dogs.

Teaching your dog to Sit, Lie Down, and Come is useful and can replace unwanted behavior. In order for your dog's training to be effective, you must practice often and the dog's response to commands must not be dependent on the environment or the presence of food. Weaning your dog off of food lures and lots of extra commands and prompting will make you both relaxed in public, because you know what to expect from each other.

If your dog's response to commands around distractions falls apart, it simply means you have more training to do. Manipulating the variables slowly in order to maintain your dog's response to commands is one key to success. If you work at it, it won't be long before you are rewarded with an obedient dog that you can take anywhere.

SSENTIALS   Consider taking a group class. The distraction of other dogs will help your dog realize that she must learn to pay attention to you. Try to make sure the ratio of teacher to student is high; twelve students to two instructors is ideal.

Self-Control Exercises

Dogs don't learn self-control unless they are allowed to make choices and are rewarded for making good ones. Using a clicker and treats to mark and reward behavior is critical. The clicker allows you to mark the right choice and begin a bank account for the right behavior. The following exercise, Choose to Sit, is one example of helping your dog learn self-control.

1. Greet visitors with the dog on a leash.
2. If the dog jumps, the visitor goes away.
3. If the dog sits, the visitor stays and the handler clicks and treats.
4. The dog learns by trial and error how to get the person to pay attention to him.
5. The handler supplies information by clicking and treating the right responses.
6. The visitor supplies consequences for not sitting by not allowing the dog to say hello to her.

As you try to solve your dog's behavior problems, keep this example in mind. Learning will last longer when the dog figures out on his own what the rewardable behavior is, especially if the dog is usually excellent in the absence of distractions but falls apart in public.

Golden
Retriever
weaving
through legs

The next exercise is another self-control exercise that helps your dog figure out how to pay attention to you. The Attention Game is intended to teach your dog to check in with you often and to ignore distractions. In time, teaching your dog to check in with you will give him a greater awareness of you, which will improve his recall and heeling commands. Dogs who have some responsibility to know where you are will not stray far away when they are off their leash. They will check in often and come back easily when you call because they know you are in control. Here's how the game works:

1. In a quiet room, sit in a chair with your dog on a leash.
2. Ignore your dog until she looks in your direction, then click and treat.
3. Ignore her again until she looks back at you, then click and treat.

4. Time yourself for one minute and count how many times she looks at you in that minute. If your dog looks at you six or more times in a minute, you are ready to add distractions.

5. Repeat this again in a new place or with a distraction and repeat the one-minute test. The distraction is too intense if your dog looks at you less than twice a minute.

6. Repeat this until your dog is looking at you six or more times a minute and then change the distraction again.

7. If your dog doesn't look at you more than twice in a minute for several repetitions, you will probably need to move away from the distraction or go somewhere less distracting.

8. Increase the quality and quantity of the rewards every once in a while to intensify the dog's response and to increase the likelihood that she will look at you more often.

9. Jackpot exceptional behavior. If your dog ignores an unexpected distraction, be sure to reward her with a whole handful of goodies to reinforce the good performance.

Your goal with this game is to increase your dog's attention to you. As a result of paying attention to you, your dog is learning to block out distractions and maintain self-control.

Having techniques and tools to help you teach your dog what is expected of her will not only make your training sessions run smoothly, it will make solving behavior problems that much more productive. Behavior problems need not be mysterious or result in the surrendering of your dog to the already overflowing animal shelters. With a little knowledge and skill you can teach your dog to be a well-behaved member of your family.

CHAPTER 10

A Word about Punishment

As humans, we are absolutely convinced that in order to change behavior we must provide some sort of punishment that will eliminate bad behavior altogether. In truth, no animals, including humans, respond well to punishment. Although it has been part of training dogs for decades, punishment is not a good or effective way to train a well-behaved family pet.

Punishment Can Make Things Worse

Over time, many trainers have found that it is totally unnecessary to use punishment in order to get reliable, acceptable behavior. In many cases, using punishment can actually make some problems worse. Consider these two points:

- Punishment stops behavior, but it does not teach or provide another choice.
- The many negative side effects of punishment outweigh the short-term benefits.

The best human example of why punishment is ineffective is a speeding ticket. If you've ever been pulled over for speeding, you'll understand. The moment the lights flash behind you is horrible. When you're actually pulled over, your heart races, you stutter and stammer, and you wait and wait and wait. Now you've got a fine to pay, and points on your insurance as well. Do you stop speeding? Well, for a little while you do, but one day you are late, you speed again, and you get away with it.

You may have been a little more careful this time, avoiding speed traps and keeping your eyes open, but you were speeding. After being punished severely only weeks before, how could you go back to that behavior? Quite simply, the punishment made you a better speeder! You are no longer a random, careless speeder; you actually look for cruisers and avoid known speed traps. The punishment actually improved the way you speed.

Punishment Is Reactive

The first problem with punishment is that it is a response to bad behavior, whereas training initiates good behavior. The second problem with punishment as a training tool is that you can't always control what the student learns. In fact, punishment puts the subject in an excitable and defensive emotional state, which interferes with the dog's ability to learn anything.

Another reason that punishment is not very effective for fixing behavior problems is that it is only part of the equation. Punishment only stops the unwanted behavior; it does not show the dog what he should have done instead. Punishment occurs too late to teach anything because by the time it is delivered, the dog has already done the undesirable behavior and cannot undo it.

ESSENTIALS

Management tools (Chapter 9) will result in a well-behaved dog without the fallout of a deteriorated relationship and the breakdown of trust that most punishment causes. Management eliminates the opportunity for wrong behavior, making it easier for your dog to choose the right one.

Punishing your dog for jumping on the company will not make him want to sit in front of them next time. In fact, punishment delivered by a visitor or in the presence of one might actually teach your dog to be fearful of visitors because it's sometimes unpleasant to be around them. This is not what you want to teach. After working so hard to make sure that your dog is social with people, it would be detrimental to all to start punishing him for being friendly.

Timing Is Everything

If you are going to use punishment and have it mean anything, the timing of the correction has to be precise; it must happen the moment the undesirable behavior begins. Not many people, especially the average pet owner, are capable of doing this. Another issue with the timing of the correction is that the dog is probably overstimulated and excited, which means her brain is not in learning mode. In order to process information a dog has to be in a fairly relaxed state.

If the timing of the correction were perfect, the dog would need to be rewarded as soon as the inappropriate behavior stopped. The timing of the reward here is the instructive part for the dog. If the behavior that we are trying to fix is one the dog has been practicing for a long time, a very high rate of reinforcement for the right behavior must be employed or the new desirable behavior will not replace the old behavior. Remember that old habits die hard, and it is difficult to adopt new ways of doing things without a being heavily reinforced for the right choices.

Once your dog is overexcited, she can't learn anything. Her behavior will either get more frantic, or she will shut down completely. The person delivering the punishment is likely to add more punishment, continuing the unproductive cycle, and no real learning happens.

Redirect the Behavior

Rather than using corrections (a polite word for "punishment), either redirect or interrupt the dog before he starts the behavior. At the first sign of alert or tension, the dog must be interrupted and redirected to the more appropriate behavior. An interruption could be something like saying the dog's name, or touching the dog on the shoulder, or turning away from whatever captured the dog's interest.

ESSENTIALS

Pay attention to your dog's levels of distraction and excitement. Overstimulation will prevent him from learning anything. Build up to working around intense distractions rather than jumping into chaos and hoping for the best.

To work effectively, interruptions must be delivered before the dog starts the behavior. In the case of barking for instance, if you wait until the dog is barking and frantic you will not be able to distract him from what he's barking at in order to teach him anything. For some one-track minded dogs, you could use a strong correction and it still wouldn't phase him or stop his behavior. It would be like trying to reason with

Golden Retriever holding the telephone

someone who is angry—a person not in a rational frame of mind is not capable of listening to you or being reasonable.

Instead, start paying attention to what triggers the barking, and interrupt the dog while he's still thinking about it. To short-circuit an undesirable behavior, you might have the dog go to his bed, or move further away from the distractions so he's not as excited. Your goal is to interrupt him close to the distractions in the environments where he practices the undesirable behavior, but it is unreasonable to try to train him there in the beginning. As with any constructive and lasting training, you need to start with small, simple steps that enable the dog to be successful.

ALERT

As you figure out a plan for what you want your dog to do, it's important to write it out and keep track of it. Make sure any treats, clicker, or other equipment are conveniently located in your house or yard, allowing you to reward your dog whenever the opportunity arises. If the alternate behavior is complicated, break it down into steps and practice with your dog frequently. Be sure to keep it simple.

Establishing New Patterns

In order to stop unwanted behavior and get your dog to develop a new pattern of behavior, you must have not only a set plan to accomplish your goal but you must also prevent the dog from practicing the old behavior while you are retraining her. Setting up a new pattern of behavior isn't easy for dogs, because they get into habits like we do and tend to do things the same way again and again if we let them.

Repetition

The important thing to remember when changing a pattern is that you need to practice the new pattern over and over and reward the dog repeatedly for the new behavior until she adopts it as her own. In the meantime, if you want to get where you are going faster, you need to stop allowing the dog to reinforce herself for the wrong behavior by preventing it from happening. Stepping on the leash to prevent jumping will not, by itself, teach your dog to sit, but it will reduce her options and make sitting more likely, because that is the only behavior getting rewarded.

An Ounce of Prevention

The more time you spend with dogs, the more you will find that a large part of training is really management. Gates, crates, and pens can be your best friends when raising and training a dog. Although they don't teach the dog not to chew the couch or pee on the carpet, they prevent inappropriate behaviors from becoming bad habits. Managing a dog's environment helps him to be right by limiting his choices. It isn't the solution to all of your behavior problems but it is an integral part of it.

When you pay attention to what's going right and ignore what the dog is doing wrong, you'll begin to reap the rewards. Dogs are social creatures that crave attention, so even negative attention when they are misbehaving may be encouragement enough to repeat the very behavior you are trying so hard to eliminate.

For example, a fence is a management tool for dogs that enjoy playing in their yards and owners who want to keep them there. A baby gate in the kitchen limits the dog's freedom so that he can't get into trouble in the rest of the house. When you don't have time to teach your dog to sit for a guest, putting your dog behind a gate would be a better way to manage his jumping problem than letting him dive on the person or run out the front door.

The Fallout of Punishment: Aggression

If punishment is mistimed or too severe, it can often cause the dog to turn and bite whoever is closest. Dogs that are corrected for barking and lunging at other dogs and people don't learn to like them; in fact, many of these animals become more unpredictable and dangerous. They learn that the presence of other dogs or people means they are about to get punished, so they will often bite without warning.

Warnings Work for a Reason

If you physically punish a dog for growling he may stop growling and skip right to the bite instead. You have made that dog far more dangerous because he no longer warns people that he is not comfortable, he just bites them. You have, in essence, created a better biter. Growling is a dog's way of warning us that he is uncomfortable and that if the person or dog doesn't go away there's going to be trouble. Punishing the warning doesn't make sense; we want to change the way the dog feels about the person or dog, not take away the warning that he is about to bite. This is nature's way of letting us know we have a problem and gives us time to do something about it (like teach the dog a positive association with people and dogs) before the dog bites.

Training Versus Punishment

Never use punishment with any problem related to aggression around people or dogs—the risk of creating a better biter is just too high. Here are five reasons to teach your dog instead of punish him.

1. Punishment must be repeated frequently to remind the dog to avoid her mistake.
2. Punishment doesn't teach the dog anything; dogs with little confidence will wilt.
3. With punishment, you can't control what the dog learns.
4. Punishment can damage the relationship between owner and dog.
5. Punishment can accelerate aggression by suppressing all precursors to aggression so that the dog skips right to the bite.

There are many reasons for not using punishment in training your dog to be a better companion. In general, punishment misses the point. It comes too late to be instructive and has the danger of teaching the dog to be better at the very behavior we are trying to eliminate.

Shetland Sheepdog targeting a plastic lid

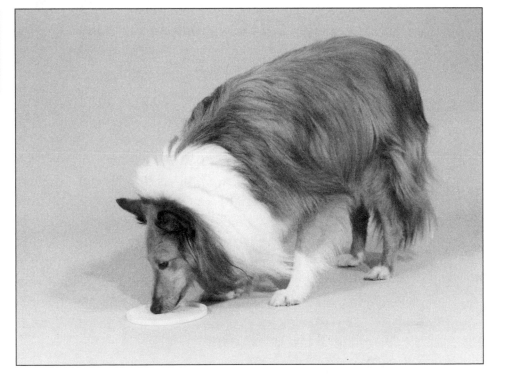

If your dog is behaving so poorly that you think she needs punishment, then the real problem is that she needs more information about what she has to do to be right. Instead of spending your time figuring out how to stop the behaviors you don't like, map out what you want the dog to do instead and retrain her.

FACTS

Aggression and fearfulness are emotional states where the dog is in a fight-or-flight mode, not a learning mode. In this frame of mind a dog is unable to learn anything. She must be comfortable, not defensive, in order to learn appropriate nonaggressive or nonfearful responses.

If a dog's basic needs for exercise, training, and attention are met and she is carefully managed according to her age and training level, you will have fewer behavioral problems and less to correct. Think carefully about how you use punishment, because it is often an indicator of a much larger issue. If you want a well-behaved dog that responds to you quickly and is fun to be around, don't use punishment to teach her; it won't get you where you want to go.

CHAPTER 11

Training a More Desirable Behavior

When dealing with behavior problems it is essential that you plan out what your dog should do in place of the behavior you are trying to eliminate. If you want to change inappropriate behavior permanently, you must replace it with the right behavior and heavily reinforce it or no real change will occur.

Have a Plan

Many dog owners know exactly what they don't want their dogs to do but very few have given much thought to what the dog should do instead. Leaving your dog with too many choices may lead to your dog choosing incorrectly and you being frustrated that he's not "getting it," which is unfair to both of you.

In order to have a dog that is trained to be responsive and enjoyable, you will need to get your family's act together. The fastest way to change your dog's unwanted behavior is to stop reinforcing the incorrect behavior and start reinforcing an alternative behavior in its place. There are endless possibilities to choose from. Sit down with your family and review the behavior questions in Chapter 9. Then, come up with ideas on how you want your dog to respond in different situations. When choosing which behaviors to reinforce you'll want to keep these points in mind:

- Keep it simple.
- Choose something incompatible with the wrong behavior.
- Plan ahead and be prepared (carry your treats and clicker with you).
- Control the variables (such as distractions and the environment).
- Avoid reinforcing the wrong behavior.
- Build a bank account for good behavior.
- Teach your dog to perform this behavior anywhere.

Every time the dog gets to practice the old undesirable behavior he is putting money in the bank for doing that behavior again. Preventing the wrong behavior from happening is half of the training.

Keep It Simple

Whatever you choose as the alternate behavior should be simple for the dog to offer quickly and reliably. Choose a single behavior, like Sit or Down, and reinforce it often. If the behavior is too complicated or involved, your dog may lose interest and go back to the undesirable behavior. A simple behavior like Sit is something you are likely to notice and reinforce even in a distracting environment. Be sure your dog knows the behavior well by applying the Ten in a Row rule.

Choose an Incompatible Behavior

Make sure that the new behavior is incompatible with the undesirable behavior. For instance, a dog cannot sit and jump at the same time. If you reinforce sitting as the desirable behavior when your dog greets new people, it won't be long before your dog doesn't even try to jump. Be forewarned: Replacing jumping with sitting takes lots of time and practice before the dog will offer it on her own. Practice in short, frequent sessions, and as opportunities present themselves from day to day. Remember, preventing jumping as an option by putting your foot on the leash will help your dog to be right more often.

Plan Ahead for Success

If you want a well-trained dog that responds to your commands everywhere, you have to train it everywhere. Dogs pick things up quickly, but are lousy generalizers, tending to revert back to old, ingrained behaviors in new environments. If you haven't taught your dog to sit when greeting strangers at the park, he will not try that as his first choice of behaviors. Always be ready to reinforce the right behavior and prevent the wrong one from happening as best you can. Have a leash hanging by the door so that you are ready to prevent jumping on guests, and have a container of treats ready to reinforce sitting.

ESSENTIALS

> In order for the new behavior to replace the old well-established behavior, it must be heavily reinforced with things that the dog finds rewarding. A reward can come in the form of attention, a game, an opportunity, or a treat—anything that the dog considers reinforcing.

If you're not prepared to train, don't allow your dog to greet the visitor. If you want to fix behavior that is deep rooted, you have to combat it with well-timed repetitions, a high rate of rewards, and frequent practice around distractions. It may seem awkward at first to carry your clicker and treats with you all the time, but it is essential to capture the moment your dog makes the right choice.

Overall, learning this way is more like real life for the dog, and the learning tends to become more permanent because the dog begins to realize that her commands work everywhere. The more distractions she gets to practice around, the quicker she will learn to generalize her response to your commands.

Lab Mix and Golden Retriever bow together

Control the Variables

Controlling the variables means controlling what's shifting your dog's attention away from you. Distractions often ruin the best-laid plans simply because they are too stimulating for the dog to ignore. If you control the frequency, type, and distance of the distractions, you will increase the speed with which your dog learns. If ringing the doorbell sends your dog into a frenzy, you may want to work on desensitizing him to the doorbell sound first; then you can move on to actually greeting the visitor. In this example, the dog's response to the doorbell and the dog's response to the person would be considered two separate issues.

Other variables might include things that move, like balls, off-leash dogs, cars, kids, runners, or environmental factors like being outside, or the presence of food. The key points to keep in mind for getting your dog to be successful around these distractions is controlling the distance between your dog and the distraction, and controlling the intensity of the distraction. In order for your dog's training program to be successful, you need to find your dogs critical distance, and work from there.

QUESTIONS?

How does "critical distance" relate to training a dog?
The critical distance is the amount of distance between the dog and the distraction that must be present in order for her to perform the behavior reliably. If she is too close to the distraction it will be difficult for her to pay attention, and she will be less likely to respond to the command.

The distance at which he notices the distraction but will still perform the behavior is the starting point. Then, in subsequent training sessions, decrease that distance until he is able to work while the distractions are close by. You will immediately notice that the distance between your dog and the action is an important factor in the success of your training sessions. If the dog is overstimulated by the distraction, he will not be able to ignore it and will not perform the behaviors you ask of him.

The second point to keep in mind when working around distractions is to pay attention to how much of a distraction you are working with. To decrease the intensity of a distraction, offer less movement, fewer dogs, people, kids, or other visual stimuli before attempting to teach the dog anything. As your dog starts to learn to ignore distractions and perform the behavior well, you can gradually increase the intensity until he is working in the middle of the distraction.

As you train your dog to respond to you regardless of where you are and what is happening, your goal over time is to decrease the distance and increase the intensity of the distractions so that your dog will pay attention to you and respond to you regardless of what else is going on.

Doing this in a slow sequence of progressions will help you attain your goals more quickly and reliably.

Prevention Is Half the Cure

Human nature is to notice what is going wrong and point it out. When trying to change behavior in animals, putting pressure upon an animal to change the choices it has made is a waste of time since the animal cannot change the past anymore than you can.

FACTS

Remember that prevention can come in the form of a leash, a crate, a gate, or a long line—anything that keeps the dog from practicing the wrong behavior while you teach him an alternate response.

If you want to make a difference in a future behavior, you must set up the animal for success. Set up an animal for success by limiting her options, providing good consequences for the correct choices, and preventing or providing negative consequences for the wrong choices. Because the animal has choices, the learning is more permanent and the consequences will directly shape her response.

Pointing out a mistake acts as reinforcement and can actually teach the person or animal to make that same mistake over and over again. A much better approach to changing behavior permanently is to avoid reinforcing the wrong behavior in the first place and if possible preventing it from actually happening. It is important during the teaching phase to avoid giving the dog any attention for the wrong behavior, and concentrate on noticing what's going right. This also means that you should be ready to reward the unexpected good behavior your dog offers anytime it happens. If you're not prepared to click and treat, then shower your pup with lots of praise and pats, or games and opportunities.

Generalization . . . Taking It on the Road

Taking it on the road means getting your dog to respond to all of his commands in new environments by training your dog everywhere.

Generalization refers to the dog being able to perform the behavior regardless of the distractions. Dogs need your help to get them on track in new environments.

The best way to help a dog whose behavior falls apart in a new environment is to go back to kindergarten. Help the dog perform the behavior with a treat or toy as a lure. The idea is to drill the dog for five to ten repetitions to get him working again and then wean him off of the extra help. Repeating the command when the dog is obviously too distracted to hear what you are saying is not teaching the dog anything but how to ignore you. With a little patience and practice, it won't be long before your dog understands that his training works everywhere, regardless of the distraction.

ALERT

When teaching your dog to generalize her behavior, a good rule of thumb is to give only one command. If the dog doesn't respond appropriately, get out a treat and help the dog perform the behavior. Repeated commands will teach your dog a slower response to commands in public places.

Solutions to Breed-Specific Behavior Problems

Dogs with persistent behavior problems are often exhibiting behavior that is related to the job they were bred to do. When a dog has a behavior problem related to its original working ability, think of it as hard-wired behavior, or behavior that a dog's genetics have preprogrammed him to do. Consider the Border collie that chases and nips at heels, the retriever obsessed with having everything in her mouth, or the terrier that barks or chases squirrels. In these cases the genetics of the dog determine her behavior, because it is a behavior that the dog was bred to do, such as herding, retrieving, guarding, or chasing things that move.

Constant and Patient Reinforcement

What hard-wiring means for you is that without the appropriate training and practice, it will be harder to stop the dog from practicing the undesirable behavior. There are several things to keep in mind when you are retraining dogs like this:

- Keep the rate of reinforcement high.
- Build up your dog's bank account for good behavior.
- Train your dog to perform the behavior for a longer period of time.
- Consider teaching a trick as a replacement behavior.

If you are going to change the dog's mind about a behavior that is this instinctive, you need to provide lots of reinforcement for the behavior you are trying to teach instead. A high rate of reinforcement means that you keep your standards low and reward the dog for even attempting the new behavior. You don't up your criteria or expect multiple repetitions; you simply reward the new behavior as often as possible. This way it will be more likely for your dog to respond to a given situation with the right behavior because it has been rewarded so frequently.

FACTS

Money in the bank is each click and treat for the right behavior. No one can ever have too much positive reinforcement for good behavior. When you are trying to change hard-wired behavior, you must increase the likelihood of the right behavior by making sure the bank account is full.

Each reward for the new behavior is money in the bank. You are building a reinforcement history that has to compete with a natural and self-rewarding behavior. Building a strong reinforcement history takes time and practice before it will eventually replace the old hard-wired behavior with the new desirable one.

Practice Makes Perfect

The more you work with your dog, the fewer behavior problems you will have. You are spending time building up a history of "training equals fun!" Teaching your dog to perform tricks is a great way to help you get to know your dog and improve your relationship with him; plus, training tricks is fun and most people enjoy spending time training their dogs this way.

Golden Retriever takes a German Shepherd for a walk

Some dogs love learning tricks more than anything else, so they are more willing to work longer and perform with enthusiasm. If you prefer to teach your dog tricks, why not use them in everyday life to help prevent your dog from practicing inappropriate behaviors. If your dog is a puller, how about mixing in Roll Overs, Sit Up, or Spin with reinforcing the dog for staying with you. In order to use tricks to replace problem behavior, not only does the dog have to know the trick very well in all different kinds of environments, she also has to be heavily reinforced (at least initially) for choosing to perform the trick rather than the inappropriate behavior. The more you practice what you want, the better it will happen for you when you truly need it. The more creative you are in your training program, the better your relationship with your dog will be.

The Bark Stops Here!

Barking can be a hot issue in any neighborhood in America (see Chapter 12). What is more maddening than listening to nonstop barking from a dog whose careless owner tied her up and left for hours? The dog's reasons for barking will determine what solution will work for your dog. Try to identify whether the dog is bored, unsocialized, fearful, or just too exuberant; then try different approaches to see what works best for you and your dog. Some options to consider:

- Hide treat-stuffed Kong toys all over the yard to prevent boredom.
- Teach your dog to retrieve a toy and carry it to the visitor to help keep your dog quiet.
- Teaching your dog to Roll Over will use up some of the energy focused on barking.
- Teaching your dog to Spin will keep her too busy to bark.
- Asking for a play Bow is a nice greeting for an elderly person or small child.
- For dogs that like to use their paws, teaching her to Wave will direct her energy appropriately.

Training your dog to use an alternate behavior will do wonders in the way of doggie PR. It will make your guests comfortable, keep you calm, and give everyone reason to reinforce your dog's good behavior with lots of love and attention.

ESSENTIALS

The best way to get rid of a barking problem is to recognize when the dog is about to erupt, and interrupt and redirect his behavior toward a more appropriate venue.

Mugging Company at the Door

Jumping is a problem most dogs do not outgrow. Dogs mainly jump in their exuberance to greet a person and to welcome them to play.

Teaching your dog an alternate greeting behavior may be an excellent solution for your dog's jumping-on-people problems.

- Require a Sit/Stay or Down/Stay before people are allowed to pet your dog.
- Ask your dog to Play Dead or Belly Up and let the visitor scratch his belly as a reward.
- Teaching your dog to Roll Over and Spin, one right after the other, is an excellent way to keep even the most energetic dog focused on his job of greeting sanely.
- Have your dog go fetch a toy to keep his mouth busy and his feet off the company.
- A Go to Bed and Stay command can save his life by keeping him away from the open door and the big wide world beyond.

Though there is no quick solution to jumping, preventing it from happening in the first place is a good start toward changing your dog's first response toward visitors. Remember that dogs do what works. If something is no longer an option, it gets eliminated from the list of possibilities and is eventually replaced by what does work. Make sure the behavior that works for your dog is something that works for you, too!

Who's Walking Who

Pulling on the leash is by far the number one complaint from dog owners and the reason that they bring their dog to obedience class. Adding tricks to your dog's repertoire will help you manage her on-leash behavior and give you more options when she starts pulling. If she never knows what you might ask her to do next, she'll be more likely to pay attention to you and less likely to pull.

Teaching your dog appropriate leash manners can be time consuming and tedious; why not break it up a little with some of these ideas:

- Play the targeting game as you walk by having your dog touch your hand or pant leg with her nose as you walk along.

- As you are walking, stop every so often and ask your dog to Spin.
- Don't walk a long distance all at once without changing direction, or frequently stopping to have your dog Sit.
- Mix up moving with Stop and Wave.
- Stop periodically and ask your dog to Roll Over several times in a row; it will take the edge off an excitable dog.

Using tricks while teaching your dog to remain under control on leash is an excellent way for her to learn to control her enthusiasm. Directing her energy toward more appropriate behavior will teach her to pay attention to you and what you are asking her to do. Remember that your dog has been pulling you along behind her for a long time. Since there is a lot of money in your dog's bank account for pulling, you'll need to counter that with huge jackpot deposits for *not* pulling. This requires frequent practice and a commitment to make sure you don't follow your dog when she is pulling you.

Fierce or Fearful

Aggression and fearfulness are two behavior problems that are stressful for both the dog and the handler. Keeping your dog from getting too overwhelmed and getting his attention back on you is your primary goal as the owner of a fearful or aggressive dog. Keep in mind that your ultimate goal is to give your dog a better association between the things he is afraid of and positive reinforcement. What better way to do that than to teach him to do tricks in situations where he normally reacts aggressive or fearfully?

- Teach him to look at you for an extended period of time on command.
- Teach him to touch your hand with his nose.
- Teach him to touch an object or a person's hand (this has to be built up to slowly).
- Teach him to Spin or turn around.
- Teach him to Bow; this may help lighten up dogs that are passing by and help your dog feel more relaxed with their presence.

- Teach him to Wave.
- Teach him to Roll Over, which will disorient him enough that he won't know where the scary person or dog disappeared to by the time he's finished.
- Teach him to say Sorry, which will flatten him into a very submissive position—a great way to diffuse other dogs.

ESSENTIALS

The purpose of teaching a fearful or aggressive dog tricks is that when a dog is performing tricks—and trained to ignore distractions—she is concentrating on something else. Think of this as another form of "incompatible behavior."

Knowing exactly what your dog needs for reinforcement is a better, more permanent way to get rid of behavior problems. Noticing what is going right and rewarding it will make it more likely that your dog will replace his old habits with more appropriate good dog manners. Remember what you pay attention to is what you get; if you start ignoring what is going wrong and start rewarding what is going right, the behaviors you see as problems now will disappear and you will be rewarded with a more well-behaved companion.

CHAPTER 12

Barking Problems and Solutions

Dogs bark to communicate with us and with each other, but excessive barking is inappropriate and a symptom of a larger problem. If a dog barks excessively it means that the dog's mental, emotional, and physical needs are not being met. This problem must be addressed first, before peace and quiet reign.

Why Do Dogs Bark Excessively?

A barking dog is a common problem among dog owners and is often the top complaint of neighbors who listen to the restless protests of a dog confined to a yard and bored to death. Dogs are pack animals with strong bonds to their family members; it is unnatural for them to be alone for hours at a time. In their boredom and frustration they tend to bark, which is self-reinforcing. Barking is an emotional release, a way for a dog to express its emotion and let out bottled-up anxiety and frustration.

A dog that barks too much falls into one of three categories: the dog that barks when left alone; the dog that barks at visitors, noise, and people passing by while you are home; and lastly the dog that barks at you for attention. Excessive barking is a symptom of a larger issue. In general it means that the dog needs something that she isn't getting or is being consistently reinforced for the wrong behavior.

Meet Your Dog's Needs

All dogs need a healthy diet, a predictable schedule, lots of exercise, interaction with people and other dogs, training, a safe place to sleep and rest, and a stimulating environment with toys and things to chew. Dogs also need to be taught from the time they are puppies to be content when they are away from you, so that they come to expect that you will return predictably to take care of their needs.

ESSENTIALS

Just like people, well-adjusted dogs are happy. Finding a healthy balance between time alone and time with people is essential for the emotional well-being of any dog.

Dogs that are with their owners all the time (perhaps you work from home or are a stay-at-home parent) can also become excessive barkers when their owners do leave them even briefly. These dogs become inappropriately bonded to their owners and in their absence find it difficult to cope with being alone. This overattachment between owner and dog can erode the dog's self-confidence and contentment when they are alone. Take a moment to examine how much or how little time you spend with your dog and make the necessary adjustments to help her feel confident and secure.

Mindful Management

The next few sections review some basic elements of what you need to keep in mind while you come up with a plan to curb (or at least cut down) your dog's barking. The philosophy is the same for training any behavior: have a plan, be patient, be consistent, and reinforce the right behaviors.

Doin' What Comes Naturally

Some breeds are prone to barking, but all dogs can learn not to bark excessively or inappropriately. If you have a dog that is known for barking, nip the problem in the bud while the dog is still a pup. Some dogs were bred for their ability to chase or guard and barking is sometimes part of the package.

ESSENTIALS

Thinking creatively about changing your dog's environment may give you a little more peace and quiet. Think about planting a row of bushes in your yard, or close the front blinds to block your dog's view of the neighborhood.

If you know what sets your dog off into a frenzy of barking, think carefully about how you can prevent these episodes from happening. The more barking your dog does the more she gets reinforced for barking. The more reinforcement a behavior gets, the more likely the behavior is to occur and become stronger. If you want to have a quieter household you need to find your dog's triggers for barking and short circuit as many of them as you can.

Set a Reasonable Goal

A dog that barks a lot isn't going to just quit one day when you find the magic cure. Barking is reinforcing to dogs and often gets worse before it gets better. Sit down with your family and set a reasonable goal for your dog. Maybe your dog is the type that barks when the doorbell rings; in this case, your goal might

Hound Mix barking

be that she's allowed to bark for thirty seconds and then she must be quiet when you tell her to be quiet. Or if she hears a noise, she can let you know something's going on but then must stop barking and go to her bed. It really doesn't matter what the goal is, so long as it is simple and fairly easy for the dog to do.

It is your job to sit down, agree on something reasonable, and teach it to the dog. Don't be afraid to set small goals and build up the time the dog is required to be quiet by seconds. It isn't reasonable to expect a dog that has been barking excessively for years to suddenly quit overnight.

Find the Antecedents to Barking

An antecedent is the trigger or the cause of a behavior. For instance, your dog barks at the sound of a knock or the doorbell. The knock or doorbell would be considered the antecedent for the behavior of barking. Knowing what triggers your dog's barking can be crucial to teaching her to be quiet. The pattern or chain of reaction goes like this: antecedent, behavior, consequence, appropriate behavior, reward. You need to complete this entire circuit of behavior in order to teach your dog not to bark excessively.

A good way to find antecedents is to keep a chart of when your dog barks and what happens right before she barks. Write down exactly what you think triggered the barking and time how long it took her to stop. If you time how long it takes your dog to calm down, you will know when you are making progress in your training program and when you are spinning your wheels. You'll know you're on track if the number of seconds it takes your dog to calm down becomes smaller over time. Good dog trainers chart progress to see results!

To change your dog's response to a typical antecedent to barking like the doorbell, ring the doorbell at random times and give the dog a handful of delicious treats or play a favorite game like tug or fetch. Your ignoring both the bell and the door will teach your dog an alternate expectation to the ringing of the doorbell.

Set the Consequences

For dogs that keep at it and barely take a breath between barks, you may want to use something to interrupt the barking. This way you will be stopping the barking for a second so that you can reward him for being quiet. A consequence is the same as punishment, so alone it will only stop the behavior—it will not teach the dog what it should do instead.

Some ideas for consequences might be a squirt of water, a loud noise, shaking a can of pennies, a nonelectric no-bark collar (this device is worn around the neck and distracts the dog by squirting a blast of citronella when she barks). Consequences would be used to interrupt the behavior of excessive barking to get the dog to stop for a second so that it could be rewarded for being quiet. You will want to plan out ahead of time what the dog should do instead of bark so that you know what behavior to reinforce.

If you just correct the dog for barking and fail to reward it for being quiet, you will get a dog that eventually goes back to barking because it isn't being reinforced for anything else. Remember, what gets rewarded gets repeated.

Notice the Right Stuff

Too often with a noisy dog, we tend to only notice when they are barking and not when they are quiet. A good part of the solution for barking is catching and reinforcing the dog for being quiet. Each reinforcement you provide for a quiet behavior will be money in the bank for a quieter dog overall. Pay attention to your dog at times like this by petting or playing with him, giving a treat, bringing him inside, letting him outside, opening the crate door, and so on. Whatever would be reinforcing at the moment, reward your dog with it and you will notice that your dog barks less over the course of several days or weeks (depending on the value of the reinforcement and the severity of the problem).

SSENTIALS   Remember that barking is just like any bad habit; it is easier to slip back into old patterns of behavior because they are familiar and sometimes reinforcing. Management and prevention is critical.

Set for Success

If you live in a busy neighborhood, be smart—letting your dog have unsupervised free access to your yard is not a good idea. He will only find things to bark at, effectively reinforcing his obnoxious behavior over and over. This poor management is money in the bank for more barking, because dogs think that barking is fun and will continue the behavior in the absence of anything better to occupy their time. Setting up your dog to succeed means that you use prevention to help your dog to be quiet, and then make sure you notice and reward him for *being* quiet. Following are some tips for setting your dog up to succeed.

Exercise. A dog can never have too much. Try play dates with other dogs, games of fetch, Frisbee, hide-and-seek, doggie day care, pet sitters, dog walkers, or anyone who will exercise your dog for you.

Occupation. Try interesting toys, bones, and chew treats that let your dog exercise his jaws. Dogs that bark are often big chewers, so make sure your dog has plenty of good stuff to chew.

Pay attention. Be there to supervise and redirect your dog. When you are present in the yard, for instance, practice calling your dog away from what he is barking at and reward him for engaging in a different behavior.

Keep him busy. Stuff hollow toys with peanut butter and dry dog food, and hide them all over the house and yard; this will give him something to do while you are out.

Remove the antecedent. Prevent barking as often as possible by blocking his view with shrubs, closing the blinds, or rearranging the furniture. Not allowing your dog to practice the wrong behavior is more than half the cure.

Meet his needs. Have a schedule and stick to it as much as possible. Hire a professional dog walker or a doggie day care to help you with walks and exercise if necessary. The more predictable your dog's routine, the better it is for him. Try to feed, walk, and play with your dog on a predictable schedule so that he will learn to trust you and feel secure.

Be ready. It is very important to be ready to reinforce what's going right. Make a plan with your family and stick to it. The more you know what you want, the more likely you are to get it.

Use a marker signal. The use of a clicker to identify for the dog which behavior is rewardable (the quiet behavior) is crucial information for the dog, and it is difficult to provide it any other way. Remember that the click marks the quiet behavior so you can then follow through with the reward.

Dogs That Bark at Visitors

Dogs that go berserk over visitors may be fearful, overexcited, or downright aggressive to people entering your home. Trying to train the dog to like visitors while also trying to greet your guest is dangerous and will probably be only limitedly successful. A new pattern of behavior is necessary to teach the dog to respond to visitors in a more appropriate way.

If your dog is aggressive or fearful of strangers, you will probably want to enlist the help of a qualified professional dog trainer or behaviorist to help you evaluate your dog and correctly identify the problem. This person will also help you set up training sessions to help your dog learn better greeting manners and be safe doing it. The biggest task to be tackled is to change your dog's mind about how she feels about company.

1. Put the dog out of the room and let your company come in and sit down.
2. After about ten minutes, let your dog out and have everyone ignore her.
3. Arm each person with the yummiest treats and have visitors drop those treats all around their feet.
4. Let your dog be the one to go to the visitor to take the treats.

Congratulations! You just performed your first huge deposit for stopping barking at visitors. Repeat this as often as you can with lots of different people until your dog begins to look forward to having company at the door. You may want to practice this scenario with your own family first, to teach the dog this new pattern of behavior and to help the family members learn a new way of managing the dog around company.

ESSENTIALS

> To speed up your dog's learning, leave a basket of your dog's favorite toys outside your front door so that visitors are armed with a toy as soon as you open the door. This will distract your dog from barking and help her develop a new habit in greeting guests at the door.

If you're not prepared to train your dog on a given occasion, remove her from the stimuli so at least you're not reinforcing the old pattern of behavior and losing ground. Putting the dog in a separate room or her crate will at least make sure she doesn't fall back to her old ways.

Friendly Options

Dogs that bark because they are happy to see company simply need a distraction to keep them quiet. Teaching your dog to grab a stuffed animal on his way to the door will keep his mouth busy and make it impossible for him to bark and hold the toy at the same time. This is what is meant by teaching your dog to do something that is incompatible with barking. A dog can't bark with a toy in his mouth.

You'll want to make sure it's a toy he really loves so that he'll want to hold the toy more than he'll want to bark. You can even leave a basket of toys by the door and let your visitor select one to greet your dog with. This will teach your dog that visitors are fun but that barking isn't part of that fun. Take advantage of any willing helpers like neighbors, fellow dog lovers, and friends. The more your dog gets to practice greeting guests quietly, the better for everyone. Take your time and experiment with different toys to see which ones become your dog's favorites and keep him so engrossed that he forgets to bark!

Taming Doorbell Madness

Dogs that burst into action at the sound of the doorbell will need some help in getting over this huge stimulus before they can be expected to be quiet. The sound of the doorbell ringing may be your dog's antecedent to barking and the most difficult of distractions for her. Most dogs with this problem explode into a cacophony of shrill barking and take several minutes to calm down.

QUESTIONS?

What is the difference between operant and classical conditioning? Operant conditioning (click and treat) recognizes, and therefore encourages, desired behavior. Classical conditioning creates positive associations between two events.

The best way to manage these dogs is to teach them an alternative response to the ringing doorbell. The easiest and noisiest way to do this is through a process called "flooding." Flooding involves ringing the doorbell a billion times when no one is there for the dog to greet so that it eventually doesn't mean what the dog thinks it means. She will start to develop an alternative response to the doorbell and come to expect something different than what she originally thought.

You can also add a bit of classical conditioning to change the dog's association with the doorbell. Classical conditioning is about developing associations between a noise or object, in this case the doorbell, and something good, like a treat or a game of fetch. To incorporate conditioning into the training, ring the bell and shower the dog with treats or start throwing a ball around regardless of the dog's behavior (barking or not).

Here, we are not requiring the dog to do something before she gets something, as in operant conditioning or clicker training. To the novice trainer, it may seem at first that we are rewarding the dog for barking when we ring the bell and treat the dog. In reality we are trying to form an association between the doorbell and something good so that eventually instead of barking, your dog will be expecting a treat, a game, a toy, or a pat from the visitor. This can be a very powerful tool in trying to change your dogs association with doorbells. Using it to help solve your barking problem may get you where you want to go faster than through other methods.

Dogs That Bark for Attention

Some dogs have their owners all figured out. Remember that most dogs don't work for a living and have nothing else to do but sit around and watch you. They know just what to do to get what they want by barking at you until they get it. When a dog barks at you for attention, it usually means that he is confused about who's in charge in the family and may not have enough rules and limits put upon him to give him a clue as to where he falls in the family hierarchy.

QUESTIONS?

Is there a trick to getting the dog to stop barking for attention?
It is important that everyone in the family be committed to ignoring the dog when he is barking for attention and absolutely not give in to the dog's demands. The more the behavior of barking at people for attention doesn't work, the faster the problem behavior will disappear.

The one thing that almost always works for these needy dogs is to stop paying attention to them when they are barking and to start noticing, marking, and rewarding them for being quiet. Walk away, turn your head to the side, or turn your back on your dog to let him know that what he is doing is not rewardable. If your dog is used to getting his way by barking, this method of management may take a while, but overall it is a faster process and more productive than constantly yelling at the dog to be quiet.

Head Halters

You will find several types of training equipment you can use to shorten your training time that gently help your dog relax and trust that you are in charge. The Gentle Leader Headcollar is one such head halter. Head halters are excellent equipment to own and with the proper introduction, they will cut your training time in half (see Chapter 15).

ALERT

Introduce the head collar slowly and with lots of goodies and positive associations. The more positively you introduce your dog to this piece of equipment, the more useful it will be to you. If you rush it, your dog's resistance will make the halter a hindrance rather than a help.

The original purpose of the head halter is to teach dogs not to pull, by guiding them under the chin. In essence, when a dog is wearing one of these you control his forward movement by controlling his head. The head halter has an added benefit, too: When fitted correctly, it puts gentle pressure on two points on the dog's head and neck, which help relax the dog and makes him feel more secure.

Some dogs find the effect so calming that they forget to bark and are overall more relaxed and mellow. Head halters should be introduced very slowly if they are to be a useful tool for you. Dogs need to be taught to wear a head halter, but once they like wearing them, it can have an amazing effect on their behavior.

Canine Massage

An often-overlooked method of achieving a quieter dog is canine massage. The massage technique most worthy of mention for changing unwanted behavior is called Tellington Touch, or T-touch. It was started on horses by a woman named Linda Tellington-Jones, and has been applied to all kinds of animals for all kinds of behavior problems.

Dogs hold a lot of their emotions in their face and mouth area, and most dogs that are tense or hyperactive tend to bark and chew to relieve anxiety. In general, dogs that are restless, overactive, aggressive, or excessive barkers often have a chewing or biting problem as well. These animals can benefit from a bit of therapeutic massage on their muzzle and gum line.

The best T-touch technique involves making small circles on the muzzle and jaw line with the tips of the fore and middle fingers. You'll want to lightly move the skin in a clockwise direction for a full circle, then pick your hand up and do another circle right next to it. Take your time and make each circle for a count of five and remember to breathe.

QUESTIONS?

Where can you find more information on the T-touch technique?
For more information on T-touch, see Appendix A for references.

You may want to start getting your dog used to this by sitting on a chair or the floor and having your dog sit between your feet. Support under his jaw with one hand while you make circles with the other. Use a light pressure, about as much as would be comfortable if you made a circle on your eyelid. You can even slip your finger under the dog's lip and make small circles on the gum line itself. You may want to wet your fingers first if your dog has a dry mouth.

There's Always Hope for the Problem Barker

Barking can be problematic for owners and neighbors alike, but it doesn't have to be. Owning a pet should be an enjoyable experience, and barking should not get in the way of you and your family enjoying your pet: the time to act is now. The longer you let your dog reward herself by getting what she wants when she barks, the more barking you will have to listen to.

Put together a training plan that will help reform your barking lunatic into the quiet companion you've always wanted. You have the tools to change the behavior, now it's time to get to work. Take the time to look seriously at the ways in which you are meeting your dog's basic needs for exercise; changing this by increasing your dog's playtime with other dogs is often a huge factor in cutting down on the amount of barking you are listening to. Most of all, don't give up. Even the most obnoxious barker can be taught to be a quieter, more enjoyable companion; he just needs to be trained.

CHAPTER 13
Fears and Phobias

A fearful dog is a challenge to own and train. In familiar surroundings he is a sweet, wonderful family pet, but in new places where there are strange sounds and people, he turns into a mess of jittery shaking nerves. If you own a dog like this, it is important to educate yourself and learn all you can in order to help your dog become a less fearful and more confident companion.

Make a Commitment to Training

Fearful dogs do not suddenly become confident, even with lots of training. Training a fearful dog to be more confident is a time-consuming project that is best undertaken with a determined attitude and clear, achievable goal setting. Being specific about how you want your dog to react and behave is a huge step toward making it a reality.

Fearful dogs operate on emotion; they are not really thinking about what they are doing, and therefore no amount of correction or comforting will help them get over it and act like they do at home. If you take on the project of working with a dog like this, you will have to learn to be patient and flexible.

When training a fearful dog it is important to be flexible; you will not always move in a forward direction. Sometimes it will feel like you move one step forward and ten steps back. Being flexible enough to realize when you've pushed too hard and being insightful enough to know what changes to make so that your dog is successful are two of the most important elements of a successful dog trainer.

Miniature Pinscher "peeking" out from under a blanket

Be Organized and Consistent

Having a regular schedule of training is important in training any dog, but it is absolutely critical when working with a dog that is fearful. Breaking your goals down into steps is the key to seeing improvement in a relatively short period of time. For instance, maybe your dog is afraid of strange men. You may start off by using a male member of your family that your dog likes and teach your dog to target the person's hand (see Chapter 4).

Targeting involves the dog approaching the strange person and touching his nose to the person's hand. This, of course, would need to be broken down into really tiny pieces if the dog is really afraid of the strange person. For instance, you may want to have the person sit in a chair and ignore the dog at first. Then, you could have the stranger drop small pieces of treats all around their feet and let your dog take his time about going up and eating them. If your dog is too scared to eat, break it down into something even easier, like having the person lie on the couch or sit a greater distance away. Your dog's appetite is a good indicator to his comfort level. If he is too stressed to eat, you need to make changes in order to see any progress.

FACTS

The amount of time you spend training your dog to target will really pay off when you start to apply it in the situations where the dog is afraid. The behavior of targeting becomes a game to the dog if you practice enough.

You would gradually change the variable so that the dog was able to eventually go and target the person's hand for a click and treat. Most people who have been successful using targeting to teach their dog to get over their fears have done an extensive amount of training teaching their dogs to target their own hands, and the hands of people the dog likes. Targeting can also be used to teach your dog to learn to be brave around scary objects or to learn to jump into the car or bathtub.

You will find that because targeting has such good associations for your dog, he will be more willing to extend himself and be open to new experiences; it will give him something to do instead of being scared. Taking the time to teach your dog how to target will be one of the most important training tools you have to help your dog get over his fears.

Genetics, Abuse, or a Lack of Exposure?

People often assumed that fearful dogs have been mistreated by a prior owner or some other person who has had contact with the dog. More commonly, however, dogs are fearful or phobic because they lack early experience with lots of different types of people, sounds, and experiences, including other dogs. Genetics can also play a fairly large role in shaping a dog's fearful behavior, and some breeds have shyness as a common, though undesirable, trait.

ESSENTIALS   It is very important to research who you are buying your puppy from and steer clear of puppy mills, pet stores, and places where they breed more than one breed.

Breeding

A good breeder is committed to turning out puppies that are healthy, well adjusted, and ready for life. They screen their potential puppy buyers and make sure they educate each person that buys a puppy so that they train and socialize their puppies appropriately. The reality is you get what you pay for, and quality puppies from good breeders don't come cheap. A lot of love and care goes into each puppy if the breeder does his or her job right.

If you feel your dog's problems stem from a genetic component, it is still possible to train her. Even in well-bred dogs with conscientious breeders, some puppies can be more fearful than their littermates. If the shyness is identified early enough, and intensive socialization and training is implemented, a lot of progress can be made in a relatively short period of time. The earlier the problem is identified, the better the prognosis. Certain breeds can be more prone to fearfulness, but any dog can grow up being fearful and suspicious of new people and experiences.

FACTS

The puppy aptitude test is a series of tests performed on forty-nine day old puppies that helps determine their tendencies to be outgoing, shy, mischievous, or pushy. More information on puppy aptitude testing can be obtained from DogWise, a dog and cat book retailer, which can be found online at ✍ *www.dogwise.com*.

A genetic predisposition to noise sensitivity is common in many breeds used for hunting and sporting purposes. Dog breeders who truly care will breed out these traits by choosing only the friendliest, most confident dogs for their breeding programs. If you are looking for a puppy of a breed that has fearful tendencies, ask lots of questions about the parents' temperaments, meet both parents before purchasing the pup, and choose a breeder who has someone perform the puppy aptitude test on all of their litters. Dogs that are carefully bred by knowledgeable, caring people should be friendly and outgoing regardless of their breed.

Social Development

If you feel your dog's fearfulness is a result of a lack of early socialization, and your dog is still under a year, get out there and get busy. The earlier you start to change this the more successful your training program will be. The longer you wait, the harder it will be to change.

Consider enrolling your dog in a well-organized group training class. Be honest with your instructor about what your goals are, and ask if a group class would be an appropriate place to start with your dog. Consider a doggie day care facility; there are often ones that take on special cases where the staff is knowledgeable about these problems. They can help make sure your dog has an enjoyable day. Don't be afraid to ask questions, and be flexible and consistent with your end of the commitment.

Getting a puppy from a person who has been raising dogs for many years and knows how to provide the right kind of environment will save you years of time in the long run. If a puppy misses out on these critical early social periods and is not raised in an environment that stimulates him to explore and learn about his world, he will be a fearful, phobic adult dog. Shyness, fears, and fear-related aggression is most likely the result of a lack of socialization than past abuse or mistreatment. Often abuse is used as the excuse for dogs that are fearful or aggressive when in reality it is a lack of early socialization that is the problem. However, there are dogs out there that have been mistreated and are fearful and skittish as a result of learning that strange people and places are scary and dangerous. The same advice applies if your dog has been mistreated; sit down and develop a plan, and then get out there and train your dog!

Young puppies have a critical window of socialization from eight to about eighteen weeks old. Socialization doesn't end at eighteen weeks, of course, but if the right amount has not been given, it will have serious side effects on a puppy's overall temperament and confidence.

Now Get Busy Training

All dogs need structure, but fearful dogs need even more. The more predictable the schedule and house rules, the better able they will be to cope with life. Spoiling or indulging these dogs will make them worse, because above all else, a fearful dog needs a strong, fair, and consistent leader. Providing structure for a fearful dog means feeding, walking, and exercising him at specific times. It means having house rules that are hardly ever broken, such as no dogs on the bed, dog must sit before going outside, or having his dish put on the floor, or having his leash put on.

No matter what your house rules are, the most important thing is that you have them. A dog that knows what is expected of her will know that someone else is going to take care of her. This alone will give her more confidence. House rules can be flexible, but not until your dog is more confident. The more strict and consistent the rules are, the quicker the dog will be to trust that you can take care of her and the more she will look to you for leadership.

Establish Rules

There are several things you can do to help raise your dog's confidence level and make it more likely that your training program will be successful.

Avoid reinforcing fearful behavior. Petting and talking soothingly to the dog or picking him up reinforces the dog for the fearful behavior. A hands-off approach where you state that everything is fine will send the message to your dog that there is nothing to fear.

No punishment—ever! There is never a reason for punishment in a situation where a dog is fearful. If a dog is frightened, she is in an emotional state, not a learning state. Physical or verbal correction will only convince her that there really is something to fear. Punishment may even bring out aggression if your dog feels threatened and vulnerable. Avoid any type of correction; it won't get you where you want to go.

Safety first. Keep the leash on at all times in public and make all the exits in your house escape-proof. Deny your dog access to the front door, for instance, if she is constantly looking to dash out the door or tends to panic during thunderstorms or with loud noises.

Exercise and mental stimulation. Dogs that lack confidence need exercise more than ever. Chasing a ball, hide-and-seek, learning tricks, agility, fly ball, or any of the various dog sports are all excellent ways for your dog to release her energy reserves and the tensions of the day.

Paying attention to providing the right environment for your dog and making sure that it is one in which she can learn to trust (because it is consistent and predictable) will put you on the road to helping your dog become a more confident and enjoyable companion.

Confidence Training

Fearful dogs don't have to stay that way forever. With lots of patience and careful training, you can help your dog enjoy life just a little more. Keep in mind, however, that building confidence in a fearful dog is time consuming; don't expect miracles overnight. Be flexible in your plans. Be sure to make room for regression, and have a plan as to how you will handle it. Being prepared for setbacks will also help your dog gain confidence more quickly, since her handler will simply shift plans and continue on rather than panic, flounder, and confuse her.

Teaching your dog to target and making a game out of it is a great way to build his confidence. If you practice enough it becomes so second nature to the dog that she will learn to play it regardless of what else is going on around her. Teaching your dog to target your hand (see Chapter 4) involves your dog bumping your hand with her nose for a click and treat. This can be a powerful tool in building your dog's confidence. Making targeting a game will give you a tool to raise her confidence level regardless of the circumstances, but in order for it to be useful you must practice a lot.

ESSENTIALS

Going slowly and building your dog's confidence gradually will be money in the bank for less fearful behavior. If you blow it and move too fast, go backwards and move more slowly or quit the session and try again another time.

Review the chapter on targeting, and once you've got your dog easily following your hand, transfer the target to another person. Find a helper that the dog knows and have her offer her hand as a target for your dog to touch. You may have to go back to the early steps and have the helper start off with a treat in her hand at first. Gradually increase the distance so that your dog will go across the room to touch the person's outstretched hand. Verbally label the behavior Go Say Hello.

Congratulations! You now have a new game to play with your dog and a way to increase his confidence around new people. Practice at every opportunity and be sure to have a backup plan in case he is too fearful to go and target. Having a plan will make it so that you will transition smoothly and your dog will barely notice that you've changed plans.

Classical Conditioning

Using classical conditioning in your training program can help you cover more ground more quickly because it deals more with associations and feelings than actually requiring the dog to perform a certain behavior. Classical conditioning involves forming an association of "scary thing" equals "good stuff." Good stuff can come in the form of games, toys, food, affection, or anything the dog finds reinforcing. Using this technique can be helpful for dogs that are just too scared to work at all or for noise sensitivities and phobias.

Golden Retriever bowing

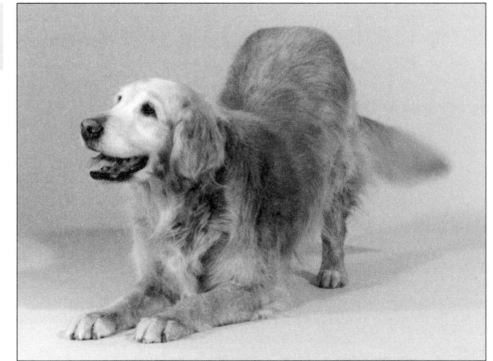

The way that classical conditioning works is that each time the noise is present, the bar is open. Throw treats on the ground, play ball, or play a favorite game. When the noise goes away, so does all the good stuff and your attention as well (ignore your dog for at least five minutes). Your goal is to change the dogs association with the feared noise to one of expecting good things to happen.

FACTS

The most important thing to keep in mind with this type of training is that the dog gets good things regardless of her behavior. Remember that you are trying to form an association between the scary person, noise, or thing and things the dog likes.

Using classical conditioning on your way to trying to change your scared dog's behavior is like making huge bank deposits in your dog's bank account. It will complement your dog's operant training program because you have a more relaxed dog to train. Half the problem of training a scared dog is that they are not relaxed enough to absorb the lesson and therefore require more repetition and more changes of variables.

Systematic Desensitization

This technique involves playing the noise at a very low volume or keeping the scary person or thing at enough distance so that the dog notices it but does not react fearfully to it. A good rule of thumb is that if the dog won't take a treat or play with you, the volume is too high or the distance is too close. Increase the volume gradually, or bring the person or thing closer, so that eventually the dog will ignore it all together and continue to take treats and play.

The process of systematic desensitization involves interacting with the dog in a positive way, be it with a game of fetch or teaching tricks, so as to help the dog develop a more positive association with the feared noise. The dog starts to associate the feeling of being relaxed around the scary noise or object and eventually the volume can be increased and the distance decreased until the dog will accept the new thing as part of his environment and no longer finds it threatening.

Teaching tricks would be a great way for the dog to associate fun with noise. If you move slowly enough you will find that having fun learning and performing tricks is incompatible with acting fearful. With enough patience and practice you will have a dog that is able to get over his fears because he has learned to trust that only good things happen.

Veterinary Behaviorist and Alternative Solutions

Veterinary behaviorists are skilled both as veterinarians and as dog behavior experts. You may consider the help of a behaviorist to help diagnose your dog's problem and help you get started working toward a solution. The main difference between a veterinary behaviorist and a dog trainer/behaviorist is that the veterinary behaviorist can prescribe medication for dogs with problems that are too intense or severe to change with training alone.

FACTS

Remember that fearful dogs didn't get that way overnight. A high rate of reinforcement (frequent clicks and treats for anything that is going right) will help you build your dog's bank account for acting confident, and this will help your dog get used to new people or things.

Consider seeking the help of a veterinary behaviorist if you don't seem to be making any progress over six weeks time or if your dog seems unnaturally fearful. Some dogs are so fearful being left alone that they will cause injury to themselves or major destruction to their surroundings in the absence of their owners. Dogs like this may benefit from veterinary-prescribed drugs that will help restore chemical balance and assist them in learning appropriate and alternative behavior. If your dog suffers from a chemical imbalance, no amount of training will change that. Restoring the body to its equilibrium will ensure that your dog will be able to make the most of his training sessions and will make progress faster. In most cases the goal is to wean the dog off the medication by adhering to a strict behavioral program until the dog learns a new response.

Veterinary behaviorists also have experience with difficult or unusual problems, like excessive tail chasing, shadow chasing, obsessive behaviors, severe separation anxiety, and aggression. A veterinary behaviorist usually charges a substantial fee, which covers the initial visit. On the first visit, the behaviorist will meet your dog and take a complete history in order to diagnose your dog's problem and advise you on the treatment.

The behaviorist will most likely design a training program for you to follow and require that you give updates on your dog's progress. In some cases the behaviorist may even refer you to a local obedience trainer to help coach you as you implement the training program. Not all problems require medication, but in some severe cases pharmacological intervention can save you huge amounts of time in training and make the success of your training program that much more likely.

Natural Remedies

If you have a dog that has complex behavior problems, it is crucial to keep an open mind about alternative methods of treatment. Not all solutions will seem to fit your problems or be something you may have even considered like massage, acupuncture, or a homeopathic remedy.

Holistic veterinary practitioners may use alternative solutions for fearful dogs. Homeopathic remedies often work to help your dog restore his natural balance so that his body can heal itself. If you do decide to go this route, the veterinarian will take a detailed history of not only your dog's heath and diet but also his likes, dislikes, and general behavioral issues. Consider seeking out a professional to consult with to see what recommendations she might have for your dog. She may use a combination of herbal remedies, body wraps, massage techniques, and behavioral training to help you achieve your goal of a more confident pet. The more alternatives you seek, the more likely you will be to find a solution that will help improve the speed of your dog's training program.

Alternative Solutions

Fear is an emotion that can get in the way of training; because of this, you may find that training alone is not the entire solution. Consider seeking out alternative methods of treatment to be sure you have covered all the bases. Often fears are the result of an injury or underlying medical problem that goes undetected and can often be successfully identified through chiropractic or acupuncture consultations.

There are also lots of different massage techniques available for dogs, including the Tellington Touch (see page 158). This type of technique helps dogs to become more confident and aware of their bodies and works well in conjunction with a behavior modification program. Regardless of what you start with, the general rule to keep in mind is to do no harm. The more open-minded you are toward trying something new, the more your dog will benefit. If you have a difficult problem, the best approach is to seek out as much information as possible so that you have lots of tools to help your dog live a more comfortable life and make him a more enjoyable companion.

ESSENTIALS

To find alternative practitioners like acupuncturists, chiropractors, massage therapists, or other types of alternative specialists in your area, try asking other dog owners, looking in the yellow pages, asking at your local health food store, contacting the nearest veterinary school, or doing a search on the Internet.

In general, phobic dogs are a mix of unfortunate experiences and a lack of early socialization appropriate for their temperament. Retraining these dogs to be more confident can be a challenge. Changing behavior that is based in fear isn't easy. It requires a huge commitment of time and energy to help your dog learn to cope with life, but the owners who embark on this adventure find the rewards immeasurable. If you are truly committed to making your dog a more confident and participating member of your family, start training your dog today!

CHAPTER 14
Housebreaking 101

Housebreaking problems are the leading cause of people giving up their animals to shelters across the nation. Nothing erodes the bond of man and dog quicker than a puddle or a pile on the carpet. Dogs have a natural housebreaking instinct that involves sleeping in a place separate from where they eliminate; we take advantage of this instinct when we housebreak them.

Why Things Go Wrong

In some cases, the puppy was not raised by a superclean mom that kept the whelping box free of stool. In other cases, the puppy may have spent too much time in a cage in a pet store or a shelter, and learned to go in her crate because there was no other option. If the natural instinct to eliminate away from the sleeping area is missing, it usually means that the puppy was mishandled and not given the opportunity to eliminate outside of the sleeping area. A puppy that doesn't have this instinct can be a lot more difficult to housebreak. This doesn't mean they can't learn to go in the appropriate place, but it will mean the whole process will take a little longer than average and require you to be more vigilant and flexible with your walking schedule.

Welsh Terrier checking out the trash

Another problem with housebreaking occurs when humans confuse setting limits with being mean or allowing too much freedom too soon. When pups have free run of the house, they go to the bathroom whenever they have to go; as a result, they never learn to hold it. Other pups are not supervised well enough when they do have freedom and sneak off to "go" somewhere inappropriate when no one is looking. Almost all housebreaking problems are caused by human error, which is good news. It means that all you need to do is educate yourself, so that you, too, can have a pooch that knows where to eliminate.

Using a Crate to Help Housebreak Your Dog

The dog's ancestor, the wolf, housebroke himself by sleeping in a cave and eliminating outside that cave. Through the adult's example, the puppies learned to do the same. We mimic this cave concept when we crate train our dogs. Using a crate is like giving your dog his own bedroom, a place for him to relax and rest without getting into trouble. Being confined to a crate requires that he hold his bladder and bowels to avoid an unpleasant consequence (having to sit in his own mess until you come to rescue him).

Using a crate gives a clear message to a puppy: "Hold it until I let you out." Such a message takes advantage of his natural instincts to sleep in one place and eliminate in another. Using a crate is the nicest thing you can do for your dog, and if it's used properly it will help speed up housebreaking. Following are some tips for using a crate:

1. A young puppy (less than sixteen weeks) should be in the crate more than she is out, and should only be free when you are there to supervise her.
2. No food or water should be given in the crate while you are gone.
3. No towels or padding in the crate at first until he's been dry in the crate for at least two weeks straight. Otherwise, he may go on the towel and then kick it to the back.
4. A puppy between the ages of eight and twelve weeks will need to be taken to the potty spot, to see if she needs to go, every hour at first and then every two to three hours after that.
5. Hire a pet sitter to provide regular walks if you are gone for long periods during the day.
6. Puppies twelve to eighteen weeks can last a bit longer between walks, but you should increase the time gradually.
7. If your pup cries or barks in the crate, try to ignore him until he is quiet before letting him out. Covering the crate completely with a

sheet or towel often helps puppies settle down to sleep faster, especially if they bark and whine a lot.

8. When introducing the crate, leave the door open and entice your puppy in and out with treats or toys. You can also use the clicker and treats to shape your puppy going in and out of the crate.

9. Put your puppy in the crate frequently when you are home so that she gets used to being away from you for gradually longer periods at a time.

10. Keep your crate around throughout the first and second year of your dog's life. You will find it a godsend if you have workmen doing repairs, company visiting, or if you travel with your dog. If you teach your dog to like his crate, he will always have a safe place to call his own no matter where he goes.

Dogs that can't use a crate for whatever reason should be supervised constantly and not allowed free access to the rest of the house until they have been reliable with their housebreaking for at least six weeks. Freedom after that should be given gradually until you are certain your dog is reliable.

Crates are not just for housebreaking—they also help keep your puppy safe while you are away and prevent destructive chewing. Though the crate may not be useful to some people as a housebreaking tool, you may find it extremely useful for getting through all of the destructive phases of your dog's development.

Charting Your Dog's Progress

Teaching a dog to use the outside for her bathroom needs is not rocket science, but it can be frustrating and time consuming. Some tricks to housebreaking won't teach your dog to go outside overnight, but they will make sure that you are moving in that general direction. A really useful tool in housebreaking a dog is to keep a chart that tracks what time she was walked, if she went, and what she did. A simple chart on the fridge will help the whole family keep track of your puppy's progress and make it easier to know when your puppy can have some freedom and when she should be supervised carefully for signs that she has to go out (most puppies will sniff the floor and walk in circles when they need to go out).

Housebreaking Habits

A young pup between seven and twelve weeks should be walked every hour. It is the repetition of being taken to the same spot time and again that gives him the idea of what he needs to do and where to do it. Pick one spot in the yard, keep him on a leash, and only stay out for about one to three minutes. If he goes, label it and play with him, or give him a little freedom in the house or yard. If he doesn't go he should be crated or kept with you and you should try again in ten or twenty minutes.

If you allow him to roam the yard on his own, chances are he will have so much fun that he will forget to go and end up coming inside and having an accident on the floor. As your puppy gets to be between twelve and sixteen weeks old, you'll find that he can go longer between potty trips. Use your chart to decide how long that should be.

ESSENTIALS

Keeping a chart will track your pup's progress, but it will also help family members know when to supervise closely and when to allow freedom. If the person who is next in charge of walking the pup checks the chart, she will know to take the puppy out more frequently and watch him closely for signs that he needs to go.

You can also keep track on your chart of when your puppy has accidents so that you will know when you need to add in an extra walk or supervise more carefully. Over several weeks of charting, you will be able to put the charts together and determine if you are making progress in the right direction, and if you aren't, what you need to do to get back on track.

No Papers Please

Using newspapers or potty pads to housetrain your puppy is the surest way to make him unreliable with housebreaking. Dogs that are trained to "go" on newspaper or potty pads never learn to hold it because they go whenever they have to. If you want to housebreak your dog reliably, don't use paper to train her. Take her outside from day one and don't look back. If you are currently using newspaper, pick it up and throw it away: start taking your dog outside today.

Using paper in the house gives your dog the impression that there is a safe place to go inside. When the paper is gone, you will have to walk her more frequently and supervise her more carefully, but she will get the idea over time that the only place she can go is outside.

Some people who have dogs weighing less than five pounds as adults choose to teach their dogs to go in a litter box rather than taking them outside. This may be a desirable option for you if you live in the city in a high-rise apartment and it is a long trip to the great outdoors. Using a litter box works on the same principles of paper training except that the actual potty spot is unique and in no way resembles a carpet or any other surface you are likely to have in your house. It would be ideal to keep this litter box on a balcony or sun porch and walk your dog as though she were going outside to do her business. If you leave the litter box indoors and allow your dog free access to it, you will have the same problems as with dogs that are paper-trained. If your dog can go whenever she wants, she will never learn to hold it and will likely never be truly housebroken.

Using a Leash for Potty Trips

Unless your dog is a rescue dog adopted from a shelter as an adult and absolutely will not go on a leash, it is a good idea to use a leash to take your dog to the potty spot. The leash should be about six feet long and you should stand in one spot; don't follow the dog all over the yard. Let the dog sniff in a circle around you and praise the heck out of him if he goes. Try not to get him into the habit of walking the neighborhood unless you want to do that in freezing cold weather or pouring rain.

The trick to walking your dog on a leash is to get him to go to the bathroom quickly without too much distraction so that regardless of the weather your dog will perform his potty duties quickly and on demand. The leash acts as a way for you to communicate to your dog that you are not outside to play but to take care of the business at hand.

ALERT

A good rule of thumb for potty trips for unhousebroken dogs is to only stay out for one to two minutes, tops. If she goes, praise and give freedom. If she doesn't go, either confine her to a crate or gated area or keep her with you for twenty minutes or so and try again. The message to the dog is "if you go, you get freedom; if you don't, you don't."

Label It, Especially for Those Rainy or Snowy Days

Dogs that are taught to go to the bathroom on cue are a pleasure to walk. Even in bad weather they go out and do their business, and their owners don't freeze to death waiting for them. Putting the act of eliminating on a cue by calling it something will help speed up the whole ordeal. The common labels for potty behavior are Go, Hurry Up, or Get Busy.

Through training, you can have each function labeled and your dog will go on command whenever you ask. This is really convenient if you're about to take them inside a store, a friend's house, or the hospital you may visit as a therapy dog team. Since you know they've gone and will last until you leave, you can relax and enjoy your visit. You can label the potty behavior by saying whatever your command is going to be as your dog is in the process of going. You can even click and treat as she is going to give her the idea that doing her business outside is a good thing. It takes a lot of repetitions for the dog to understand that the command means to "go," so be patient and make sure everyone in the family knows what commands are being used.

Make a Potty Spot in Your Yard

You may also want to consider creating a potty spot in your yard, a designated place where your dog can do his business without interfering with the beauty of the rest of your yard. Creating one area that clearly says "bathroom" to your dog will not only help you housebreak him, but it will also keep him from using the whole yard as his toilet. That way if you'd like to have barbecues or you have children that play in the yard, you won't have to worry about scooping the whole yard.

To build the potty spot, you'll want to use materials that offer good drainage and the ability to disinfect. Here are some potty spot recommendations:

- Make a square or rectangular box out of garden timbers cut to the dimensions you wish. Large dogs probably need an 8' × 8' area, whereas smaller dogs could probably live with a 4' × 4' space.
- Cover the bottom with several bags of sand.
- Cover the sand with a variety of sizes of crushed stone. Some people prefer the tiny size often called "pea stone"; others prefer the 1-inch diameter.

Designated potty spots will allow you to scoop easily and disinfect with a bleach solution regularly. A weed sprayer with a 30:70 solution of bleach and water works well as a disinfectant. Even in tight quarters, this arrangement eliminates excessive odors and unsanitary conditions. A metal rake may also help you to redistribute the stone and sand.

Confinement Works

Young puppies, or even adult dogs, that are not housebroken should not have free access to the house. If you allow too much freedom too soon you will create housebreaking problems. Dogs often consider where they eat and sleep their home and the rest of the house the outside. That is why a puppy kept in the kitchen will often run to the dining room and piddle or poop if he gets loose. Using a crate to keep your puppy confined when you cannot watch him is an excellent housebreaking tool.

ESSENTIALS

The confinement area should be relatively small, to keep the puppy from designating one end for sleeping and the other for the bathroom.

Try not to put any cozy blankets, newspaper, or bedding inside until he has proven himself by staying dry in the crate for two weeks straight. For dogs that cannot be crate trained for some reason, confinement by means of baby gates is key. If the dog is walked on a regular basis, he will do his best to keep his gated area clean.

Control the Food and Water

A puppy is like a sieve: what goes in will come out. Pay attention to how much and how often she eats and drinks, and regulate what goes in so you can regulate what comes out. Your unhousebroken dog should not have free access to food and water, because she will eat and drink whenever she wants and you be less able to predict when she'll need to go out. In order to housebreak a dog, you need to stick to a strict food and water schedule and be sure that she is walked at regular intervals. Puppies that have a regular feeding routine are easy to predict; if you feed and water them on a schedule, they will go out on schedule.

The best way to help a puppy develop a reliable housebreaking schedule is to feed roughly at the same time each day and not leave water out all day and night. Put the food down for ten minutes; then pick it up if he doesn't finish and put it away until the next meal. Feed a young pup seven to twelve weeks old three times a day, and feed an older puppy or adult dog twice a day. Put the water down at regular intervals and pay attention to how much he drinks. Remember: what goes in comes out.

Don't Punish Your Puppy for Mistakes

An important aspect of housebreaking a dog successfully is to reward success rather than punish mistakes. Mistakes are really your fault for not walking your puppy at the right time. If you'd like to hit yourself over the head with a rolled up newspaper, feel free! Your puppy will not learn not to go in the house by being scolded or punished. What she will learn is to avoid going in front of you and instead go under the dining-room table when no one is looking. The end result is that it will be nearly impossible to get her to go on a leash, because she will come to believe that going in front of someone is wrong.

FACTS

Providing a consequence for unproductive trips to the potty spot is a good idea. The most logical consequence is a lack of freedom. A dog that normally goes at a certain hour, like first thing in the morning or last thing at night, should not be allowed to play freely in the house or yard until he has had a productive trip outside.

Deal with mistakes by ignoring the pup for a while. Put him in a crate or gated room, clean up the mess, and make a note of the time of the accident. Keep track of your dog's mistakes to see if there is any pattern to them and if you should add in extra walks.

Proper Cleanup Procedures for Accidents

When your puppy has an accident on the carpet or floor, it is essential to clean it up as quickly and as thoroughly as possible to eliminate any lingering odors, because any remaining smell will draw the puppy back to that spot. Here are some tips for cleaning up urine on carpet:

1. Blot up as much as possible with paper towels.
2. Pour an eight-ounce glass of water over the spot to dilute the urine.
3. Blot with more paper towels until there is no hint of yellow on the towels.

4. Spray carpet cleaner over the entire spot and scrub with a brush or a sponge.
5. Spray the area again and follow the product's directions for standing time and vacuuming. (Repeat as needed.)
6. Spray with an enzyme inhibitor, which eliminates the odor, following product directions exactly.

FACTS

If you are not sure you know about all the spots where your dog has gone, consider purchasing a black light (available in some dog supply catalogs) to detect the urine stains on the carpet.

Cleaning up urine or feces on hardwood floors should be done a little differently to prevent permanent damage to the floor.

1. Wipe up excess with paper towels.
2. Mix up a bucket of Murphy's Oil Soap and water and wash the area thoroughly with a mop or sponge.
3. Dry the area thoroughly with a rag or paper towels.
4. Spray an enzyme inhibitor (made especially for this purpose) on a cloth and wipe down the area one last time.

Cleaning up feces on carpet can be tricky. Be sure to remove as much as possible with paper towels before treating the area to avoid rubbing the excess into the carpet and thereby compounding the problem.

1. Remove all solid waste with paper towels.
2. Spray with carpet cleaner and rub out as much as possible with a sponge.
3. Spray the area again and use a scrub brush to deep clean the fibers of the carpet.
4. Spray the area with carpet cleaner again and follow the product's directions for standing time and vacuuming. (Repeat as needed.)
5. Spray with enzyme inhibitor (available in most pet stores) to permanently eliminate the odor.

6. If your dog tends to continue to go back to the same spot over and over, consider rearranging the furniture a bit to block access to that spot.

Cleaning any area where an accident occurred is essential to keeping your dog on track with his housebreaking. If you are cleaning up more than a couple of accidents a week, you are probably not walking your puppy outside often enough or are allowing too much freedom too soon. Remember that limiting a puppy's freedom is half the key to housebreaking and is only temporary until your puppy proves he knows where to "go" and is completely reliable.

ESSENTIALS

Cleaning up accidents efficiently is very important. A dog's sense of smell is intense; if accidents are not cleaned up thoroughly, it can draw the animal back to that spot time and again. Many great products on the market today help not only to clean up the mess but also to neutralize the odor, making it less likely that your dog will be drawn back to the same spot.

Dogs need to go out at least once during a four-hour period if confined to a small area, like a crate. If they have more freedom or free access to food and water, they may have to go more frequently. Most adult, housebroken dogs need to be walked first thing in the morning, sometime midday, after work, and before bed. A midday visit from a pet sitter can help your adult dog maintain his excellent housebreaking manners.

A lack of housebreaking is a silly reason to give up a dog to the shelter or pound, but living with a dog that uses your house as her bathroom is no picnic either. Housebreaking manners are the most basic of training issues that must be accomplished if a dog is going to live peaceably with humans. The tricks to housebreaking come down to some very basic elements; confine the dog in some way, put her on a schedule and keep track of her successes and failures, control the food and water bowls, walk her outdoors in short, frequent spurts, and avoid punishing her mistakes. If you follow these guidelines your dog should be making fairly good progress within a month to six weeks' time.

Shetland
Sheepdog
sitting

Occasionally a dog may have a medical problem that is interfering with housebreaking. If you were making good progress with housebreaking but your dog suddenly regresses, consider having your veterinarian check a urine and stool sample for signs of infection or parasites. Both of these medical conditions can be easily treated with medication and will often present themselves as a regression in a housebreaking program.

It is silly to pursue an issue behaviorally if the real problem lies in a medical condition. If, despite your best efforts, you find your dog's housebreaking problems baffling or you adopted your dog late in his life and he came with a host of serious behavioral problems, you may want to consider the help of a professional dog trainer or behaviorist.

CHAPTER 15

Pulling on the Leash

I f there is a common problem among dogs, it is pulling on the leash to get where they want to go. From the biggest Great Dane to the tiniest Chihuahua, all dogs regardless of their size learn to pull on their leashes from an early age.

The Only Solution Is Training

Leash pulling doesn't seem to be such a big problem until you try to walk around the block with a dog that thinks she's the lead dog in a sled team, determined to reach the dog park in record time. Pulling on the leash is one of the major reasons people stop taking their dog's for walks—it takes all the fun out of a leisurely walk around the neighborhood when one of your arms feels as though it is being pulled out of its socket.

QUESTIONS?

Why do dogs pull?
Dogs pull because it gets them where they want to go. If every time your dog leaves the house she is allowed to hit the end of the leash and you follow her wherever she pulls you, you are reinforcing the behavior and letting your dog think it is okay.

If you look in pet stores and in pet supply catalogs, you will see dozens of devices that supposedly magically stop your dog from pulling. The truth of the matter, however, is that dogs will continue to pull until you teach them to stop, regardless of the equipment you are using. Only you, as your dog's trusted companion, can choose what method you want to use to teach your dog to walk with you instead of drag you, and there are many options out there that you can try. The key to any training program, however, is *you*—how much time you invest in the project and how consistent you are about sticking to it until the job is done.

Define Your Terms

Whenever you want to fix any behavior problem, it is a good idea to sit down and figure out what you would like your dog to do instead. In this case, it is important to define how you want your dog to behave on leash. Do you want her to walk at perfect heel position or is a loose leash sufficient? Where exactly would you like your dog to be, and what will it look like when she's there? Will your arm be relaxed or extended, is sniffing okay, and which side should she be on?

Narrowing down what you are looking for gives you a better idea of what you are going to reinforce and will help you recognize it and reward it. Only by reinforcing the right behavior will you be able to get rid of the undesirable one. If you don't know what your dog has to do to get the reward, you will not be successful at getting rid of pulling and teaching him an acceptable alternative. Sit down with your family now and decide how you want your dog to behave on leash.

ESSENTIALS

A good barometer for heeling is to pay attention to the slack in the leash. Look at the arm that is holding the leash: if your elbow has a bend in it, the dog is walking with you nicely; if your arm is straight, you've got some training to do.

Lack of Exercise Contribution

Nowhere is a lack of exercise more apparent than when a dog is on leash. A dog with few outlets for his energy will pull, spin, and tug on leash to get where he wants to go. Giving your dog appropriate outlets for his energy, such as playing with other dogs, swimming, and playing fetch, will help give you a more calm on-leash companion. Active dogs need at least thirty minutes to an hour a day of flat-out running to take the edge off of their energy. Without this outlet you can expect behavior problems. Exercise is part of a dog's basic needs for mental, physical, and emotional stability and to ignore this fact is to set your dog up for failure. If you don't have the time to exercise your dog to the point of fatigue, consider hiring a pet sitter, dog walker, or doggie day care professional to help you give your dog the exercise he needs. Trying to train a dog that is not getting enough exercise is a project in frustration and should be avoided at all costs.

Walk Without Pulling

Teaching your dog to walk at your side rather than pull your arm off requires lots of practice and repetition. This is not a behavior that is going to change overnight. Remember that pulling works, or has worked, for quite a long time for most dogs, and behavior that gets reinforced gets repeated. A huge step in the right direction is to stop following the dog when the leash is tight and she's pulling you. This may mean suspending all walks around the block so that she doesn't have the opportunity to practice pulling.

Managing your dog's behavior by not allowing her to practice it isn't teaching her to walk next to you, but it's a step in the right direction since she isn't being reinforced for the wrong behavior. Following are some tips for teaching loose-leash walking:

- Walk at a brisk pace and change direction frequently so that your dog has to pay attention to where you are going. The more turns you offer, the more your dog has to pay attention to where you are.
- Once you get the hang of walking and turning frequently, start to pay attention to the moment your dog turns to follow you, and click and treat him for catching up to you.
- At first, you may want to stop walking for a moment after the click so that the dog realizes what exactly he's getting clicked for. Use really delicious treats that your dog loves to keep his attention focused on you.
- Start off practicing in a distraction-free place, and gradually go to busier places when your dog starts to understand what you want.
- Attaching a six-foot leash to your waist will keep your hands free for this exercise, so you will be able to click and treat your dog when he is next to you. Remember that the message you are sending to your dog is that pulling does not get him where he wants to go because when he pulls in one direction it makes you go the other way.
- For most dogs, the faster you walk the better, since a steady pace forces them to pay attention to where you are going next.
- Using a clicker to mark the behavior of being next to you will shorten your training time by half. The clicker tells the dog exactly what he's doing right to earn the reward. The clicker is clearer and more precise than any other tool you can use.

When you want to change a behavior that has been working for the dog for quite some time, you need to reinforce the right behavior often and with a high-value reward. Your dog has been pulling to get where she's going for as long as you've had her, so in order to get rid of pulling you must replace it with a behavior she finds more rewarding. In order for her to choose to walk next to you over pulling, you will have to do lots of repetitions with yummy rewards.

SSENTIALS   Remember that you are building your dog's reinforcement history for loose-leash walking. If you are going to do this effectively, both the rate of and value of her rewards has to be high.

Really great reinforcements can take the shape of treats like cheese, freeze-dried liver, roast beef, or chicken, or favorite games like tug or fetch. Whatever the reward, the dog has to want it more than she wants to pull. Be creative and fun and your dog will soon be trotting happily next to you.

Adding Duration to Your Walks

From a training standpoint, duration refers to the amount of time your dog can maintain the requested behavior. In this case, it's the length of time that the dog has to be next to you in order to earn his click and treat. Once your dog starts to catch on to getting clicked for coming back to your side, you can then raise the criteria to his coming back to your side and staying there for a step or two. Eventually you will build the length of time the dog must walk next to you to several minutes, until the dog no longer wants to pull. Remember, duration refers to the length of time the dog must do the behavior before he gets rewarded. Practice having him walk with you for different lengths of time around a variety of distractions until he can trot happily next to you under any circumstance.

Changing the Variables and Distractions

Practicing in a new environment—with people, dogs, cars, bicycles, and other distractions—is critical to the reliability of the behavior. Changing too many of these variables at once, however, will make your dog's behavior of walking next to you fall apart. To help your dog to learn to stay with you despite the distractions, change one variable at a time. The variables involved in heeling refer to how close or far you are to the distractions and how intense the distractions are (one person, a crowd, kids, adults, people with dogs, wildlife, cars, bikes, and so forth).

By controlling the variables and working slowly to introduce distractions while you maintain your dog's ability to walk at heel, you will teach your dog to walk nicely on a leash regardless of the distractions in the environment. Don't ever be afraid to stop the training session and make it easier for the dog to be right if things are going badly and your dog could use some extra help.

FACTS

The length of time you choose should be random so that your dog does not pick up on a pattern. It is probably best not to increase the length of time all at once but instead to skip around with low numbers and then gradually increase the time as the dog catches on to the game.

Controlling Heeling

There are two major variables involved in teaching your dog to heel: the distance to the distraction and the intensity of the distraction. The distance between your dog and the distraction is too close if you can't get the dog to perform the behavior. If this is the case you should back away from the action to a point where your dog will perform the behavior well. Once your dog is working well, you can decrease the distance between your dog and the distraction, bringing her closer to the action when you are sure your dog can handle it.

Setting your dog up for success is the key to becoming a good dog trainer. Here are some ways that you can set your dog up for success.

- Reduce the intensity of the distraction (quieter, slower, less of it) as needed.
- Use your best treats; training is difficult, so make it worth his while.
- Offer a high rate of reinforcement in a new environment.
- Slow the rate down (click and treat less frequently) for longer versions of the behavior (dog stays with you longer), and when the dog starts to be able to perform the behavior reliably.

Choose what distraction you will start with and set it up so that your dog can be successful. The intensity of the distraction has to do with its speed, noise level, and quantity. The intensity is too high when your dog can't perform the behavior because he is too distracted. The solution to this problem is to tone down the distraction by making it go slower, quieter, or having less of it.

Common Distractions

Another consideration when you are working your dog around distractions is the type of distraction you are working on. There are three major categories of distractions, things that move, things that smell, and things that make noise.

1. **Things that move.** This category incites your dog's prey drive, her desire to chase after things that move. Every dog has a different level of distractibility, but most dogs find things that move irresistible. Examples include cars, bikes, squirrels, runners, dogs, motorcycles, balls, or kids.
2. **Things that smell.** The majority of dogs are motivated most by their stomachs, so for the hunting breeds especially, the "nose to the ground" behavior can be quite a challenge. Examples are food, animals, other animals' feces, and wildlife.
3. **Things that make noise.** Some dogs are more sensitive to sound than others. The average dog that is simply curious will get over it quickly and learn to ignore sounds if you change the variables, distance, and intensity slowly.

Always be sure there isn't a physical reason why your dog won't walk with you. Check his feet for cuts, make sure the pavement isn't too hot, or that his feet aren't stinging from salt-treated roads in the wintertime.

Distractions need to be worked into the training gradually. If distractions are too frequent or intense, the dog will get overexcited and be unable to concentrate, and no real learning will occur. It is important that you pay attention to his excitement level and tone down the distractions so that he is able to absorb the lesson.

The Mule Impersonator

Laggards often plant their butts and will not move forward. They will not move or follow you with any amount of coaxing or cooing. There are several tricks you can use to get these dogs to follow you:

1. Put tension in the lead but don't pull. Make sure the leash is hooked to a regular collar, not a training collar.
2. As soon as your dog takes a step toward you to steady herself, be ready to click and treat and lavish with praise (some dogs take a while, so be patient).
3. Repeat this every time your dog stops. Don't go back to her; simply ignore the wrong behavior and pay attention to the right one instead.
4. Within ten minutes or so most dogs give up their stubborn-mule impression and go with you. Some dogs may need you to do this over several sessions before they give up.

Use Grand Rewards

Teaching your dog to heel can be time consuming and boring—for both of you—if you don't come up with ideas to make it more interesting and fun. One way to make things more fun is to hide the rewards all around your training area before you start your session. It will be such a surprise to the dog to be rewarded with a delicious treat or an awesome toy that she wasn't expecting to be pulled out of the bushes. The element of surprise will make you far more interesting to your dog, and it will make your dog much more willing to learn to walk with you.

QUESTIONS?

Can scared dogs learn to ignore new sounds and walk at heel? You can train any dog to walk at heel. For the scared dog, it would be best to teach him to deal with novel noises and build his confidence first. Once he loses his skittishness, then try to teach him to heel around such distractions.

You may also want to consider using a variety of rewards paired with the click. Some examples are a game of tug, a game of fetch, a stuffed toy, a fantastic belly or flank rub, and lots of excited praise. You can teach your dog that you are interesting and full of great surprises by hiding your goodies everywhere and keeping your dog guessing about what you're going to pull out next.

Training Equipment

Training collars, head halters, and other devices are just that: devices. Their purpose is to manage pulling while you are teaching your dog to heel. The goal should be to have your dog learn to heel with the help of a training device and then to wean the dog off that device and have them heel without it.

Collars and Leashes

You can find several training devices that keep dogs from pulling. The most common are the regular slip collar or choke chain, the pinch collar, and the head halter. The slip collar works by restricting the dog's airway for a fraction of a second and making it unpleasant for him to pull. The pinch collar works by pinching the skin around the dog's neck and making it unpleasant to pull. The head halter works by pulling the dog's head downward, making it impossible to walk until the dog stops pulling and walks closer to the handler.

As with any device, you must teach your dog the step-by-step process for heeling, and in most cases this should occur before you start using the device itself. After the dog has learned how to get rewarded, the use of a training device will help you sort out the various distractions. Special situations, such as the veterinary clinic, may require extra management before your dog is completely trained. No one device is right for every dog, but the head halter is probably the most useful for most dogs.

No device will "teach" your dog to heel. You are the one that must break down this leash-walking issue into simple steps that you can incorporate into training a little at a time. The training devices will help you manage behavior, but that is all.

Head-Halter Benefits

There is one particular name brand of head halter, the Gentle Leader Headcollar, which tends to fit better than others available on the market today. It has two adjustable straps: one for the neck and one for the muzzle. The leash clips underneath the dog's chin. Think of the way a halter on a horse fits and you'll have an idea of how this works. The principle behind why the head halter is superior to other training devices is that it controls the dog's forward movement by controlling the dog's head. You would never expect to move a horse by pulling on its neck for instance, but you can easily move a 1,200-pound animal in the direction you want to go by guiding it by its head—well, at least most of the time!

This same principle works for dogs. The head halter is not a muzzle— the dog can still eat, catch a ball, and bite with it on, and no dog should be left unattended while wearing it. If your dog should try to bite or eat something he shouldn't while wearing the head halter, you can easily close his mouth by gently pulling up on the leash. The pressure that exerts will easily close his mouth and pull his head down, effectively preventing him from continuing the behavior. The head halter is sometimes described as self-correcting, meaning the handler does not

Hound Mix wearing a Gentle Leader

have to pull on the leash or yank the dog in any way to get him to stop what he is doing. It is also important to note that if you choose to use this device, you should attach only a six-foot leash to it, never an extendable or retractable one. If your dog were to take off after something and hit the end of a long leash while wearing a head halter, he could injure his neck. Introduce the head halter over a period of about two weeks. The longer you take to make this fun for the dog, the more useful a training tool it will be.

The introduction of the head halter should be a gradual process, whereby you slowly teach the dog that wearing it is fun and means good stuff is about to happen. Your goal is to make him as excited to see the head halter as he is to see his leash. Using a clicker and the yummiest treats, introduce the head halter by following these steps:

1. Show the halter to your dog and click and treat her for sniffing at it.
2. Open the nose loop and click and treat your dog for poking her nose through it to get at the treat.
3. Once she's eagerly putting her nose through the loop on her own, give her a good-sized treat and while she's chewing, fasten the neck strap.
4. Let her move around a bit and click and treat her for not pawing at her nose.
5. If your dog gets the nose loop off, take the whole thing off and leave her alone for ten minutes or so. Completely ignoring her will make her all the more eager to work with you again. The idea here is that she will want to keep the halter on because you pay extra attention to her and give special treats only when she has it on.

6. Later, when she isn't pawing as much, attach a leash to the clip under the chin and repeat steps 4 and 5. You will have to go back and click and treat her for walking without pawing at her face every time you introduce a new distraction or variable.

7. You are now ready to use the head halter on your walks, but go slowly. Take your dog for a short walk, and click and treat her for walking outside without pawing at her face. Keep the walk to no more than five minutes long.

8. As your dog gets used to wearing the head halter in public, you can gradually increase the distractions, the length of time you walk her, and any of the other variables.

Remember to make it easy for the dog to be right if you notice any regression around distractions. This is especially common when other dogs are present. The head halter can be a wonderful tool for helping you manage your dog around distractions and teaching her not to pull, but introducing it takes time, so don't rush your dog.

ALERT

Think of the head halter as a guide. Use it to guide your dog on her walks. Never pull, snap, or correct your dog in the halter, as it could damage her neck or spine.

If this device isn't useful for a dog, it is usually because the owner rushed the introduction because the dog seemed to tolerate it fairly well. Don't be fooled—just like with training other things, you get out what you put in. The following are tips for making this work for you.

• Be patient during this introduction. The head halter is a more useful tool if you introduce it slowly and let the dog learn to like wearing it (up to a week or two).

• You will have no need for jerks or pops or corrections with a head halter; in fact, doing so can injure a dog's neck or spine.

- Make sure you read the halter's directions carefully before you use it on your dog. It's important that you teach your dog to wear it and avoid letting him lunge or pull while wearing it.
- Lunging or pulling can injure your dog's neck or spine, causing him discomfort and long-term medical problems.
- If you have trouble, find a qualified positive trainer to help you introduce this piece of equipment to your dog.

Teaching your dog to walk without pulling is a time-consuming task, but it is well worth the effort. Having a dog that will walk politely beside you without yanking your arm off makes him a more pleasant companion that you won't mind taking anywhere with you. Remember that you need to build your dog's bank account for not pulling through lots of practice and consistency. At the very least, stop letting him practice the behavior of pulling by stopping every time he hits the end of the leash. By using the right equipment, introducing distractions slowly, and controlling the distance, you will gradually teach your canine companion that walking with you, rather than dragging you, is the better alternative.

CHAPTER 16
Running Away

Dogs that don't come when they are called have learned that getting away from you is rewardable. If they run off and find things to eat, roll in, and play with, then running away has huge benefits and it doesn't give them much incentive to come and be with you.

Why Do Dogs Run Away?

When the average person calls her dog, she puts the leash back on and goes home, or crates the dog and goes to work, or puts the dog in the car and drives away. Since it normally isn't beneficial for the dog to come to his owner, because his owner doesn't provide a very rewarding consequence, the dog chooses to reward himself and run away.

The difference between a trained dog that comes when called and an untrained dog that doesn't is based on the dog's perception of who controls what he wants. Dogs behave in ways that benefit them, so the key to having a dog that is always willing to come when called is making it worth the dog's while, regardless of the distraction. Trained dogs know that their owners hold the keys to everything they want, and the rule is that the dog must do something to get it.

Use a Leash to Control the Variables

The most important thing to remember is that every time your dog takes off and has a good time she is putting money in her bank account for not coming back. Don't allow an untrained dog off leash in an unsafe area or an area where she will be difficult to catch. A dog that has an unreliable recall is a danger to herself. She doesn't have good judgment and will often run in the street, get lost, or eat something harmful. If you love your dog, use a leash in unfenced areas so that you do not give your dog the opportunity to run away.

ESSENTIALS

When you use a leash to teach your dog to come, you are using it to limit her options. The fewer options she has, the more likely she is to be right and choose coming to you over running away to please herself.

Keeping your dog on leash gives her the ability to be right more often and allows you to reinforce those choices, making it likely she will choose you again and again. When you eventually get to the point where you are not using a leash anymore, it will be easy to get rid of it and still have the same level of behavior. Since you have not used the leash to teach her to come by yanking on it, but instead used it to merely limit her options, you have made it more likely that she will choose you over the distraction.

Make Sure the Rewards Are Worth the Effort

Your dog needs you to use the best possible rewards if he's going to choose coming to you over pursuing a distraction. Remember that a squirrel, cat, child, or another dog is a thrill to chase, bark at, or sniff around. If your dog chooses to be with you over the distraction, make sure you have the best treats, toys, or games as the reward. You will mark your dog's behavior of turning in your direction with a click and follow it by a treat, a game, or an opportunity to interact with the distraction (but only after checking in with you first). Using rewards in this way is not a bribe; you are simply requiring that your dog check in with you before he gets what he wants. For dogs that learn this game, it almost completely eliminates the desire to run away. Using rewards in this way means you control the dog's access to what he wants and you pay up when he checks in with you.

QUESTIONS?

How can I speed up my dog's response to Come?
Using a reward that your dog really likes can make the difficult task of coming when called more fun and rewarding for the dog. Experiment with different types of food, toys, games, and opportunities, and see how it affects your dog's performance.

Ideas for Rewards

Making the rewards variable and exciting will enhance your dog's performance and make the process of teaching your dog to come all the more fun. Here are some things to keep in mind when you are considering different types of rewards in your training program.

- Food rewards can include cheese, liver, chicken, beef jerky, tortellini, hot dogs, roast beef, and steak.
- Toy rewards can include stuffed animals, balls, tug toys, Frisbees, etc.
- Games rewards like fetch, tug, and Frisbee can help a high-energy dog stay focused on you and redirect the energy that would have been used to chase the distraction.
- Real-life rewards include the opportunity to chase the distraction (a ball, a squirrel, a leaf), to go say hello to the person or other dog, to go play with the group of dogs off leash nearby, to go swim in the pond, go plow through the snow, roll in the smell, or whatever.

ESSENTIALS

The best way to use a nonfood reward is to limit the time you interact with the dog after the click to a few seconds if it's a game, or use the real-life reward at the end of the session as a way to reinforce to the dog that coming to you is just the most terrific thing ever.

Leadership Matters

Ninety percent of a dog's recall has to do with who's in charge. Dogs with firm, strong leaders almost always come when called because you are in charge of everything great and your judgment is worth trusting. Being a leader does in no way imply being a bully or making your dog do something; in fact, true leaders never have to force a dog to do anything. Leadership is about setting limits and having rules about what is allowed and what is not allowed. Having guidelines is essential if your dog is going to do as you wish.

Quite simply, a strong leader controls resources that the dog wants access to, including his dinner, the outdoors, attention and affection, and space (including sleeping places). In a nutshell, leadership entails being first, being more powerful, and being in charge. Your ideas and decisions rule, not the dog's.

Being the leader means that you control the resources that the dog wants. It does not mean, under any circumstances, that you dominate or bully the dog in any way. Here are some guidelines for you to review:

1. Nothing in life is free. Your dog must do something to get something.
2. Respond quickly to commands. Pick a number of seconds that you'll give your dog to respond to the command; if he doesn't respond on the first command within the time frame you've chosen, he doesn't get whatever you were about to give him.
3. No dogs on your bed. No dog, let alone a dog with a behavior problem (especially a recall problem), should be allowed to sleep on the highest, most privileged spot in the house: your bed.
4. Leaders go first through doorways and up and down stairs. Teach your dog to wait and let you go first.
5. No dogs on the furniture; your dog should be on the floor or in her crate or bed.
6. Leaders control space and move about without interference. Don't step over or around your dog; if he's in your way, make him move.
7. Leaders initiate attention and games. Pushy dogs that hound you with toys or nudging should be ignored until they give up. You can call them to you later when it's your idea to play.

FACTS

When you require that your dog earn privileges, you are in charge. When the dog gets them for free, he doesn't need you and won't trust your judgment. Controlling whatever it is that the dog wants is the key to controlling the dog's behavior.

You, as the leader, can control what your dog wants by controlling his options and what he's allowed to have. The rule is that when you are experiencing behavior problems you need to be strict about allowing privileges and having house rules. When your dog behaves in a more acceptable way in a few months' time, you can relax some of the rules here and there without losing your status as leader. Think of it as similar to allowing a child to stay up later in the summertime. Staying up later in the summer is a special thing for a child; once September comes, she knows she will have to go to bed at the usual time.

ALERT

If you are strict at first you can relax your rules later and allow your dog privileges without losing ground. Having rules is essential for a dog that is content and relaxed. Just like children, dogs take comfort in the fact that someone else is in charge so that they can enjoy just being dogs.

Building a Foundation for *Come*

The foundation for Come is the most important part of the exercise. It requires that your dog turn away from the distraction and look back at you (and eventually move toward you as well). The Come command is really a Leave It command, because the dog has to turn away from what it wants and come back to you. The more reliable your dog is about turning away from the things it wants, the better able you will be to get her to come to you anytime, anyplace. If you teach a strong foundation for self-control (see Chapter 9), Come will be easier to train, and your dog will be reliable anywhere you take her. Although you have already taught Come to your dog (see Chapter 5), take a moment to review the shaping steps again:

1. Stand with your dog on a leash and don't let her get to what she wants; when your dog turns away from what she wants and looks back at you, click and treat.
2. If it takes your dog more than a minute to look back, you are too close to the distraction; back away.
3. When the dog is turning in your direction easily, run backwards as she turns to look at you and let her catch you. Click your dog as she is moving toward you and put the treat at your feet.
4. Practice putting the treat between your feet, so when she takes it, it will be easier for you to catch her.

5. Practice handling your dog's collar and leading her by it, clicking and treating her for tolerating being led by it.
6. Label the behavior Come when you have the dog by the collar.
7. Change the environment and distractions, practicing in various places.
8. Use a longer leash, twelve to twenty-five feet, and repeat from the beginning.
9. Let your leash drag until your dog proves she understands the command.
10. Vary the size and type of rewards to keep the dog guessing as to what she'll get as a reward.

Change Old Patterns

Old habits die hard, and a dog that consistently runs away to entertain itself is practicing the very opposite of the behavior you are trying to teach her. If your dog has run away a lot in the past and gotten away with rewarding itself again and again, you are going to have to put in a lot of time to prevent her from running away and reward her for coming with really memorable rewards.

ESSENTIALS

Don't miss opportunities to reward your dog for good behavior Even if you are not directly training your dog to Come, reward your dog for any amount of checking in with you. This in and of itself sometimes is enough to get the check-in behavior started.

Some dogs refuse to come to you because nothing good happens when they do. For instance, just before you leave for work, you call your dog in from the yard, put him in his crate, and leave him there for eight hours. Or at the park, you call him away from his dog friends and then put him in the car and go home. Try to change this setup by calling him several times before you actually need to leave and allow him to go back to playing as the reward. Changing *your* pattern of behavior (calling the dog and putting him back on leash, for instance) may be harder than you think.

Miniature Pinscher coming out of her crate

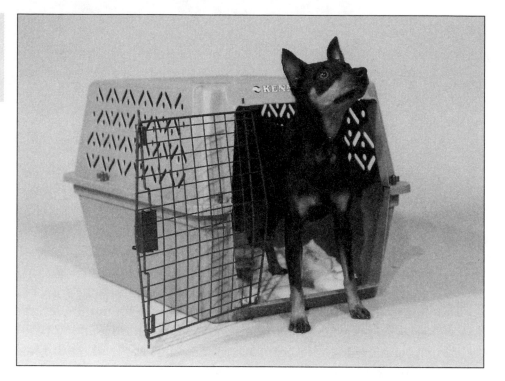

Again, having a plan of action—what you desire and what you will reward—will make training easier. Prepare ahead of time how you are going to react, and you will be rewarded by a dog that is much more likely to come to you than run away and reward itself.

Keep Recall Positive

Punishment only stops the undesirable behavior, it doesn't teach the dog anything. By the time you've punished your dog for running away, you have him back. In his mind, you are punishing him for coming to you, making it unlikely that you'll get him to respond enthusiastically in the future.

Remote punishment through the use of electronic collars is also not appropriate in the hands of the average pet owner. Even when used by professionals, such devices can teach the dog to be distrustful and fearful of her environment. It is much safer and more reasonable to teach your dog what you expect of her and avoid punishment altogether. When it comes right down to it, punishment misses the point; it is almost always issued too late to be instructive and if it isn't delivered with perfect timing, it will have absolutely no positive effect on the dog's behavior. Use your time and energy wisely—teach the dog what is expected of her instead of punishing her for making a mistake.

FACTS

Teaching your dog that the consequences for coming when called are good is the best way to have a reliable recall. A good consequence could be a few minutes of attention and affection from you, a really good treat or game, or the opportunity to go right back to what you called him away from.

The Importance of Exercise

The more exercise your dog gets, the more likely he will be to come back when you call him. A dog with no opportunity to run and explore will be less likely to return to you on demand. Make sure your dog gets to play and run for at least thirty minutes to an hour (or longer!) every day. Ideally, he should exercise and wrestle with other dogs; if interactive play isn't possible, chasing a ball, swimming, or other energy-expending pursuits are a must.

If there is an easy way to put a dent in the solving of a behavior problem, this is it. Almost any professional dog trainer will tell you that a tired dog is a good dog! Backyard confinement doesn't count. Most dogs don't want to be by themselves, and without a companion they will often bark, howl, chew, and escape the confines of their yard. Meaningful interaction is the key to engaging the dog's mind and body and making sure that his needs for exercise are met.

Play hide-and-seek with your whole family and take turns letting the dog find you. Call him back and forth to you in the yard or in a big field or at the beach (have him drag a long leash if you think he'll take off). Play fetch, blow bubbles for him to chase and catch, or take him swimming. Whatever activities you choose, get out and get active, and enjoy your dog and the great outdoors. I bet you will find that providing more exercise makes your dog more likely to stay closer in the great outdoors.

Consider this: The more time *you* spend exercising your dog, the better you'll feel, too! All levels of the relationship between family and pet benefit from the time you spend together.

Safe Confinement

You can confine your dog any number of ways, but it's important to pay careful attention to details so that she can't escape. Keep in mind that no dog should be left unsupervised outdoors unless you have an absolutely escape-proof, locked, chain link run. You can call a fence company to come and design a dog pen to fit your needs, but keep in mind that dogs that are confined outdoors tend to develop barking problems.

If you build your own pen, you must keep several things in mind during design and construction. Ideally, you should bury ¼-inch mesh wire about three to four inches under a gravel base; that way if your dog decides to dig, she can't dig out. Watch your dog carefully to make sure she doesn't eat the gravel. There are several options you can consider for the bottom surface of the pen. A cement slab may be a good choice if there is adequate shade, but it is not the most comfortable surface to lie on in extreme weather conditions (either hot or cold). One very effective solution is concrete patio block (or pavers) surrounded by crushed stone. The size of the stone can be whatever you feel would be best for your dog.

Depending on the size of your dog pen, you could put some kind of doghouse or shelter at one end, use patio block for half the length, and leave the rest just plain stone. This arrangement makes it easier to disinfect the pen, keeps the smell to a minimum, and is attractive to look at. A locked gate is essential to prevent anyone from stealing your dog. It is really not a good idea to leave your dog unattended, but in circumstances where you need to be gone for an extended period, a pen will at least give your dog a chance to relieve himself in an appropriate place.

Invisible Fences

An invisible fence is a buried wire around the perimeter of your property provides an electrical barrier that prevents your dog from leaving your yard. To keep your dog within the confines of the yard, your dog wears a collar that gives it an electrical correction if it crosses the barrier. The biggest problem with these fences is that they do not prevent people or animals from coming onto your property, which is why you should never leave your dog unsupervised in an invisibly fenced area.

Invisible fencing lets you restrict your dog's access to certain areas, like swimming pools, driveways, or decorative gardens. In order for this kind of fencing to be used humanely, your dog must be taught to respect the barrier. Hire a qualified professional dog trainer to help you teach your dog where the boundaries are and how to avoid getting corrected.

ALERT

There is some controversy regarding invisible fences and the type of correction they give the dog, and whether or not that correction is humane. The bottom line, regardless of opinions, is that you must do what you feel is best for your dog.

Although this book promotes positive training methods, if someone can't afford to fence their yard properly, an invisible fence is much better than doing nothing. Not using preventative measures increases the risk of the dog getting lost or killed. Keep in mind that some dogs are not bothered by the electrical correction and will run through it. A physical barrier in the form of chain link or solid wood is a better choice for dogs like these.

Front-Door Safety

Making sure your dog doesn't slip out the front door is essential to keeping her safe. Try to prevent front-door escapes by thinking ahead and perhaps denying access to the door through which your dog is most likely to escape. Tighten your screen door so that it closes more quickly, or put a baby gate that locks in the doorway to prevent escapes. Teach your children to be mindful of where the dog is when they are coming and going. Put your dog in a crate or gated room when there are a lot of kids and adults coming and going. Family parties and holiday gatherings are notorious times for dogs to escape and get hit by cars. When you have less control of the home environment, pay special attention to your dog's environment; prevention is half the cure.

ESSENTIALS

Your first job is to teach your dog that looking back at you is the best way to gain access to the things she wants. If she has this basic foundation, your chances for a successful recall will be greater.

Spend some time teaching your dog appropriate door manners, like sitting and staying without going through the door (even if it's wide open) until told to do so. This requires lots of on-leash setups with a helper to hold the leash in case your dog tries to make a break. You'll want to practice at first with the door shut and then gradually build up to your dog holding the Stay while you open and close the door. You can even increase the difficulty by actually going through the door and leaving the dog in a Stay. The key point to remember here is to reinforce the dog for holding the Stay, not coming through the door. Make sure you practice often and provide a high rate of reinforcement for the right behavior.

Teaching your dog reliable recall is probably a more complicated task than you ever imagined. It is not strictly a training issue, but a relationship and management issue as well. Teaching a strong foundation for Come is essential to getting your dog to realize that you are worth paying attention to even in a new environment. Once you have accomplished this reliably, your job will then be to change the variables and get your dog to perform the basic task of looking back at you around all different kinds of distractions. In addition to investing the time it will take to teach your dog a reliable recall, take the steps necessary to create a safe and limited environment that he can enjoy.

CHAPTER 17
Jumping on People

A common behavior problem that dog owners have to deal with is their dogs jumping on people. Sometimes the owner of a jumping maniac may stop having visitors because the jumping is so intense. Jumping is natural, for certain breeds, but your dog must function acceptably both in your home and in public.

Why Do Dogs Jump?

Jumping up on people is one way to get attention, and since dogs do what works, the problem can perpetuate itself to the point where the dog jumps constantly. It is important to understand where jumping comes from and what causes dogs to do this unlikable behavior. Dogs in a pack situation greet each other face to face, and after a few licks and sniffs they have decided whether they are friend or foe and proceed from there to fight or play. When they have been away from their group for a prolonged period of time, they greet each other with a combination of licking and sniffing to re-establish their status within the group and find out where their family members have been.

QUESTIONS?

What about people who invite my dog to jump?
Being consistent is a very important part of training. Be clear about what the rules are and be a strong advocate for your dog. It is imperative that while you are teaching your dog an alternate behavior, no one, however well meaning, sabotages that plan.

When pet dogs jump on us, they are trying to get to our faces in order to greet us in a similar manner. This natural behavior, which is actually a gesture of affection and happiness, can easily scare or offend strangers—or owners—resulting in the dog being isolated from the very people she is trying so hard to be with. Dogs that are exuberant greeters need to be taught appropriate manners around guests so that they can be part of family life. After all, jumping works: it gets people to pay attention to them!

The Welcoming Committee

Many people don't like it when their dog jumps on them and place a lot of emphasis on how to stop the behavior of jumping. In truth they are barking up the wrong tree. It is far more effective to define what you prefer the dog to do instead. It is more likely that you will reach your goal if you know what behavior you are looking for so that you can reward your dog for performing the right behavior.

Emphasizing what you want the dog to do by noticing it and rewarding it will help you achieve your goal of a better-mannered pet. Most people choose to have their dogs Sit and Stay when they say hello to people; this is a clear goal for the dog to accomplish and can be used in place of the jumping behavior. You should teach your dog how to Sit and Stay and reinforce it generously when she offers it around people.

Build a History

Rewarding your dog for the right behavior over and over makes the right behavior a more likely choice when your dog is faced with greeting new people. Dogs do what works; if sitting is rewarded when he greets new people, he will try sitting as his first choice. This is where knowing what you want your dog to do comes in handy. If a Sit/Stay is what you want the dog to do instead of jump on guests, then you must reinforce it often and handsomely.

The way to change unwanted behavior is to heavily reinforce appropriate behavior and keep your dog from practicing the wrong behavior as much as possible. For instance, when a guest is visiting, keep a leash on your dog so that you can step on it whenever necessary to prevent your dog from jumping. Click and treat the dog anytime she sits without being asked to. Have the guest go away and try again, but this time, ask for Sit only once. If it happens, click and treat; if it doesn't, the guest goes away. The dog learns by trial and error that if she wants the visitor to stay, she must sit and if she doesn't sit, the guest will leave.

If your dog has only a vague idea of what Sit and Stay mean, it is essential that you review with him somewhere where it is quiet and there are few distractions. You can't expect a dog that can barely Sit and Stay where there are no distractions to Sit and Stay when there are people to jump on.

This exercise assumes that you have taught your dog to respond to the Sit command and you have practiced it in all different environments with lots of different types of distractions. Apply the Ten in a Row rule to see if your dog really knows how to Sit in each new environment. Do this by asking your dog to Sit ten times in a row without a click or treat (you can praise each correct repetition). If he doesn't get ten out of ten correct, you have more training to do. Go back to drilling and practicing with him with this distraction until he can pass the test.

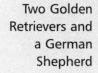

Two Golden Retrievers and a German Shepherd

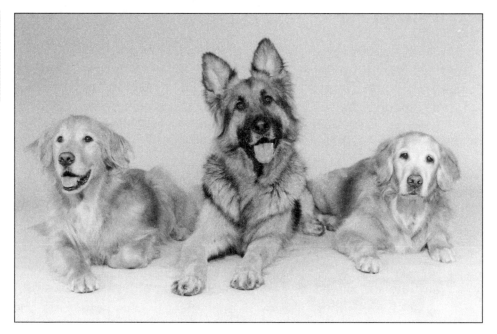

Provide Lots of Opportunities to Practice

There is nothing like repetition to aid the learning process. The more opportunities the learner has to practice the desirable behavior and get rewarded for it, the more likely the learner is to offer this new behavior in real life. Making short interesting training sessions—with lots of changes in variables and delicious treats, toys, and games as rewards—will set you on your way to having a dog that knows what to do and does it because you have taught him. Setting up lots of training sessions where you practice different types of greetings will help your dog gain the experience he needs to have good manners anywhere.

Lots of different things are happening when a dog is learning how to greet people without putting his paws on them. Changing these variables slowly enough to maintain the dog's response to the command, yet with enough variation to challenge him a bit, is the key to successful training. Every session will take you that much closer to your goal of a well-mannered pet. Some of the training scenarios for teaching or practicing a polite greeting are:

- A person greeting you and your dog while you are out on a walk
- A visitor at the front door
- A person greeting your dog at the pet store, the vet, or the groomer
- A person with a dog greeting you and your dog
- A person sitting somewhere and you and your dog approach them
- A person walking up to you while you are sitting with your dog
- A child greeting your dog
- A person with food greeting your dog

The more combinations of variables that you train for, the more reliable your dog will be and the more likely he will be to offer a Sit/Stay behavior instead of jumping. The key to having things run smoothly is to not change more than one variable at a time. Don't be afraid to go back and review Sit/Stay in places your dog has never been or places where he has a history of jumping and obnoxious behavior. Start off in places where you can get your dog's attention easily, and gradually build up to places that are very distracting for him.

FACTS

When trying to get rid of undesirable behavior you must consistently set your dog up to succeed. Limit her options, give her every chance to get it right, and reward her when she does. Setting your dog up to succeed will help your dog learn what is expected of her and make her a more pleasant companion to have around.

Define Your Dog's Greatest Distraction

Figuring out what makes your dog lose control in different environments will help you break your training sessions down into smaller pieces, making it easier for your dog to be successful. It is important that you do *not* try to train your dog when she is totally out of control, because she isn't thinking about learning or paying attention. It is a more valuable use of your time to take it slow and add in one distraction at a time until your dog learns to ignore all distractions and stay focused on you instead.

Take a minute to think about where you are likely to meet people when you are out on your walk and try to determine the circumstances around her jumping. Does your dog go crazy when she meets new people while you are out for a walk? Are they passing you on the street or approaching you while you are sitting somewhere? What scenario distracts her the most, and what are the circumstances leading up to it? Some of the distractions that dogs find irresistible are: company at your front door, your children coming home from school, your relatives visiting, and people with dogs at the park. Defining the circumstances around which your dog loses control is useful since it gives you an idea of where to start and what you will be working toward.

ALERT

Just as your dog did not start jumping overnight, he will not just suddenly stop. Taking the time to recruit your family and friends as mock guests will allow you to set up training sessions that mimic real life and let your dog learn that he must Sit and Stay in front of people instead of jump on them.

If your dog is totally out of control around people who come to the door, for instance, you could break down the distraction for your dog into smaller pieces. One of your training sessions could start by practicing Sit and Stay in front of the closed door with no guest; then you could add a family member as the guest; then put the family member outside the door; then add a knock or the doorbell; and eventually build up to being able to practice this with real guests. Breaking the hardest distractions down into small training sessions that introduce one aspect of the distraction at a time is the key for helping your dog to learn a new response in a stimulating environment.

If your dog is more of an outdoor kind of jumper that gets overexcited in play and starts mugging you for the ball, using a leash might help you manage this behavior while you reward him for doing something more appropriate instead. When the dog is excited, ask for Sit once. If he sits, click and throw the ball; if not, tell him "too bad" and walk away for a minute or two and try again after a couple of minutes. The click marks the behavior of sitting on the first try, and the dog's reward is the toss of the ball. What better way to teach your dog some self-control than to make the throwing of the ball dependent upon his response to the Sit command. Once he catches on, even a really energetic dog will love this game. Using games is a great way to enrich your relationship with your dog while fine-tuning his response to basic obedience commands and general control issues.

Avoid Punishing Jumping

Punishment is tempting and seems to work at first because initially the behavior of jumping goes away. But really, all punishment does is stop the behavior temporarily; it does not instruct the dog to choose the right behavior, nor does it replace jumping with anything but the prediction of being punished. Putting this kind of emphasis on punishment for jumping can backfire with sensitive dogs, making them afraid to greet people and suspicious of hands or knees. Dogs that have aggressive tendencies may actually turn and bite the person that is correcting them, causing a much more serious problem than the one you started with. Remember that punishment comes too late to teach the dog anything, and if poorly timed may teach your dog that visitors mean he's about to get punished.

Instead, set your dog up to do the right thing: Sit instead of jump. Make sure you notice him when he's not jumping and reward him with lots of attention! A wise trainer once said, *you get what you pay attention to.* Start paying attention to what's going right and the good stuff will start happening more than you ever imagined.

Some dogs actually view yelling, scolding, or pushing as a reward—because, after all, it *is* attention. Any attention for the wrong behavior will perpetuate that behavior and make it stronger.

Remember to Manage the Behavior

Part of every training program to fix behavior problems includes management. Management isn't training so much as it is prevention. You are preventing the dog from practicing a behavior that drives you nuts. Part of managing jumping might involve keeping your dog in another room when guests arrive until you are ready and able to train her.

Even if you only perform minimal management, you should be putting your foot on the dog's leash to prevent her from jumping anytime there are people around. Each time you fail to do this and your dog jumps on someone, you are putting money in the bank for this behavior and it will become stronger with time. Keep a leash by your front door for ready access whenever visitors arrive. Have your foot on your dog's leash anytime you go into the pet store or veterinary office or stop to talk to a neighbor on the street. The fewer opportunities your dog has to jump on people, the more swiftly she will learn to sit instead.

Teaching Sit/Stay with Duration

The duration of a behavior refers to how long the dog has to do the behavior in order to get reinforced. To avoid jumping, you want the dog to Sit and Stay for an extended period of time. You'll want to extend this period of time slowly until your dog will hold the position without trying to jump for one to two minutes. Eventually you'll also want to have your dog perform the Sit/Stay despite the distractions of people or other dogs.

Although you learned how to shape behavior for Sit/Stay in Chapter 5, take a moment to review it for these circumstances:

1. Use a treat to lure her nose upward and move your hand slightly back.
2. When her bottom hits the floor, click and treat.
3. Repeat this until your dog is offering Sit readily when she sees your hand above her head.
4. Practice without the treat in your hand. Click when her bottom hits the floor and follow up with a treat.
5. Put the treats off your person and repeat, running with the dog to go get the treat after you click for her bottom hitting the ground.
6. Introduce distractions or train somewhere new and go back to the beginning if necessary.
7. Change the variables to mimic the ones that happen in real life: people visiting at the park, on the street, at the pet store, as well as at home.
8. Build duration in a nondistracting environment and increase it to double the amount of time you'll think you need. To build duration, simply count extra seconds between clicks and treats until your dog is easily waiting twenty to forty seconds for her click and treat.

Building in a long duration for Sit/Stay will help you in public when there are lots of distractions. In practice you may be working on thirty seconds and in real life your dog may give you only fifteen seconds, but it's a start. Even fifteen seconds will give you time to react quickly enough to keep your dog from putting her paws on a visitor.

Creating a Sitting Maniac

It isn't hard to get a dog hooked on a behavior that works, but it does take time and thought along the way. One great activity to keep things interesting for puppies is the Sit for a Treat game. To play this game in a group-dog setting, take your dog off his leash and wander around the room greeting other puppies. Approach one of the other puppies with your dog and have the owner of that puppy ask her dog to Sit, asking only once. If the pup sits on the first try, click and treat and move on to the next dog. If the puppy doesn't sit on the first try, simply walk away and ignore the pup, moving on to the next one. Sometimes if the puppies are very high energy it takes awhile for them to catch on, but pretty soon several pups will be sitting perfectly in the middle of the room while the rest are running all willy-nilly around them. One or two lone pups may be sitting stoically, refusing to move for anything—they know exactly what they need to do to get people to pay attention to them.

Boston Terrier lounges on her bed

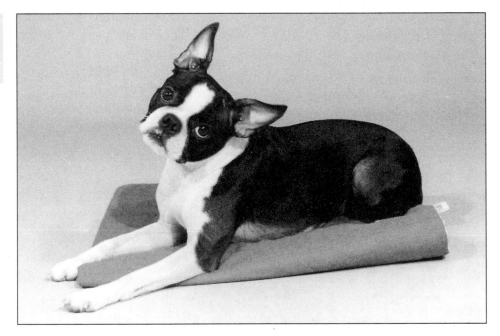

Play this game at home by inviting a bunch of family or friends over and doing the same exercise. Have everyone wander around, armed with clickers and treats, and take turns giving only one command to Sit and clicking and treating your dog for responding on the first try. Pretty soon, you will see your dog going from person to person, sitting as fast as his rear end will let him to earn his goody. Use your dog's dinner for this exercise if you'd like; it's a great way for him to practice his good manners and earn his dinner doing it.

Jumping is a natural behavior gone astray through inappropriate reinforcement of the wrong behavior. There is nothing difficult about teaching your dog to Sit instead of jump, it just needs to be practiced in increasingly distracting environments until your dog adopts it as second nature. Remember, as with any bad habit or addiction (yes, some dogs are so good at jumping that they have become addicted to it), it takes time and patience to change unwanted behavior. Through lots of repetitions and opportunities to practice the right behavior you will find that your dog will be sitting for attention instead of mugging people. Owning a dog that knows how to greet guests politely makes it easier to take your dog anywhere and have him actively involved in your life.

FACTS

The absence of reinforcement for undesirable behavior can be a powerful message. Dogs expect the people they jump on to acknowledge them in some way. Train the people in your family to turn and walk away from your jumping dog without any contact.

CHAPTER 18
Dogs That Dig

Does your backyard look like an archaeological dig? Some dogs dig huge craters that resemble a dirt swimming pool, while other canine archaeologists prefer to leave dozens of smaller holes conducive to ankle breaking. Regardless of your dog's digging style, most dogs find digging a pleasurable and self-rewarding activity, and once they get going it can be hard to stop them.

Why Do Dogs Dig?

Most of the terrier breeds were bred to dig out vermin, mice, rats, and moles, and so for some dogs digging is instinctive. Generally, however, dogs dig for a variety of reasons, ranging from boredom, frustration, and lack of exercise to a real need to stay cool on a hot day. Looking at some of the reasons for digging might help you get to the bottom of your dog's digging problem.

Boredom

A bored dog is a ticket to destruction. A dog with nothing to do will bark, howl, chew, destroy, and dig. Digging is a great stress reliever and digging up whatever treasures she can find is well worth the effort. If you think that boredom may be your dog's motive for digging, take steps to improve her environment now. Provide lots of safe, interesting toys, and rotate them regularly. Take her for a romp in the woods, play with other dogs at the park, or teach her tricks. Anything you add will help alleviate some of the boredom that is causing her to dig. A great way to alleviate boredom in addition to physical exercise is mental exercise. Some ideas for mental workouts are:

- Stuff Kong toys with dog food and peanut butter and let your dog figure out how to get the food out.
- Freeze the toy to make this an even cooler challenge on a hot day.
- Invite a friend's dog to spend the afternoon playing and wrestling with your dog.
- Buy interesting toys for your dog and rotate them weekly so that your dog always has something new to play with.
- Put treats in all different places in the yard for your dog to find.
- Put your dog's meals in a treat-dispensing toy and let him work for his dinner.
- Put peanut butter or cream cheese on the inside of the shaft of a marrow bone (uncooked) and let your dog have a blast licking it out.
- Make some agility equipment—tunnels, ramps, jumps, etc.—and teach your dog to negotiate them with and without your help.

Remember that dogs need a variety of play, training, and exercise to be happy, healthy, and content family pets. When any behavior is extreme, like digging or barking, it usually is an advertisement for needing more of something. In most cases it's that the dog is bored and frustrated because she does not get enough exercise or one-on-one time with her owner.

Frustration

If your dog is unsupervised in a fenced yard or dog pen, he may start to dig out of frustration. Your dog can see and hear people passing by but can't get to where the action is. A dog that is frustrated by being confined for too long will often try to dig his way to freedom. Don't leave your dog unattended for long periods of time, and stimulate his environment by hiding toys packed with his dinner and peanut butter or hiding bones and things to chew in the area where he is confined. Go out and play with him and distract him away from digging if he does it while you are present.

FACTS

Playtime with other dogs is a great stress buster and an essential part of the day for the average active dog. Invite a dog friend over on a regular basis to help you tire out your active dog, or consider enrolling your pooch in a well-run doggie day care.

If your dog tries to dig out of the yard, you may want to bury ¼-inch mesh wire along the fence line to make it impossible to dig past a certain depth. Most dogs get discouraged once they hit something that won't let them dig any deeper, and find other pursuits. The best way to alleviate frustration is to spend more time with your dog and provide him with more things to think about.

Exercise

If there is one thing that can save you time in the long run, it's providing your dog with enough exercise. The more opportunities your dog gets to run, chase, swim, wrestle, roll, and romp, the less energy she has to dig holes. If you own an active dog, and most diggers are very active, she will need at least one to three hours of exercise daily. Whether you take her for long runs in the woods, allow her off-leash time to play with other dogs, or enroll her in a doggie day care program, she needs her exercise. Make sure you're doing what you can to meet her basic needs before you complain about the digging.

Provide Shade

Not paying attention to a dog's basic need to be cool on a hot day may contribute to your dog's digging problem. On a hot day, a dog's instincts tell him to find a cool, dry place to rest. In the absence of adequate shade, a dog will often dig a hole and lie in it. Digging a hole to lie in is a natural way for the dog to cool himself on a hot day. If your dog is outdoors in hot weather, provide plenty of shade, shelter, and water, or consider leaving him indoors with the air conditioning on or a fan running. All dogs have a different sensitivity to heat and cold; observe your dog for signs that it's too hot or too cold for him outdoors. Here are some ideas for keeping cool on a hot day:

- Give your dog a frozen Kong stuffed with peanut butter and his dog food.
- Set up a beach umbrella and a kiddie wading pool in the yard.
- Put some ice cubes in his water bowl.
- Freeze some dog biscuits in water and put them in the wading pool.
- Get a special sun-reflecting tarp and secure it over your dog's outdoor pen.

For the sake of his comfort—and health—you need to provide your dog with plenty of water and shade on hot days. Make sure that even an active pooch is not allowed to overdo it with play and exercise. Try taking your dog out for exercise early in the morning or after the sun goes down to prevent heat stroke.

Legal Digging Zone

Dogs whose genetics tell them to dig need alternative outlets for their enthusiastic escapades. Replacing the inappropriate behavior with a more appropriate one is the only permanent solution. If digging comes naturally to these dogs, why not provide a safe, legal place for them to dig by making a digging pit. A digging pit can be any size, but 4" × 4" for small dogs and 8" × 8" for larger breeds can be a general guideline. Use garden timbers to make a box shape and fill the box with sand. You may actually want to dig out the existing soil and make a bed of stone for the bottom to supply good drainage. This way, regardless of the climate, it won't become a mud puddle in inclement weather. Fill the rest of the pit with play sand, the kind used in children's sandboxes. Use a metal rake to evenly distribute the sand.

ESSENTIALS

You may want to invest in a metal rake so that you can clear any uncovered treasure from the digging pit and keep the sand loose and inviting. You may also want to add fresh sand periodically to provide plenty of places to hide new goodies.

Now comes the fun part! Bury toys, bones, rawhide, dog cookies, balls, and other surprises for your dog to find. Make some of the treasures easy to find, others more difficult. The more of a digger your dog is, the more challenging you should make the treasure hunt. Periodically (once a week) you should hide new treasures and rake the pit to remove any old cookies, bones, or other treats. You may want to make a pit out of a child's sandbox for dogs that stay in a chain link run while you are away. Be creative in what you bury and your active dog will know exactly where to dig to find the good stuff. Here are some ideas for buried treasure:

- Hard dog cookies
- Kongs stuffed with peanut butter and treats
- Marrow bones (real ones from the butcher, uncooked, is safest)
- Rawhide sticks, bones, chips
- Pig ears smeared with cream cheese inside a paper bag
- A small cardboard jewelry box filled with treats
- A cardboard ice-cream box with treats or a chew toy inside
- Hide a favorite toy, like a ball or a stuffed animal, in a paper bag and bury it

Regardless of the treasure, be sure it is something that your dog can safely have unattended. Experiment while you are watching him to be sure he doesn't eat anything that he shouldn't (like the paper bag that you've hidden the tennis ball in). A certain amount of shredding is fine, you just don't want him eating the entire empty ice-cream container.

QUESTIONS?

What about filling in existing holes?
There are many theories about what to do about the holes that your dog has already dug. Some people leave the holes alone and the dog only digs in the holes he's made. Other people put large rocks in the existing holes before filling them in. Experiment and see what works best for your dog.

Two solutions for digging that work for some folks are to bury some of the dog's poop in each hole, or bury ¼-inch mesh wire about one to two inches under the soil. In the first case, the dog uncovers something she thinks she's buried before. In the latter, when she hits the mesh, she can't go any deeper and gives up.

Regardless of what you try as a solution to stop your canine archaeologist from turning your yard into the Grand Canyon, the only way to really stop a digger is not to give him the opportunity to dig in inappropriate places. Supervise him closely, don't leave him unattended in the yard, and consider building him a digging area of his own. A dog that really enjoys digging will love the opportunity to practice it legally. You'll notice that there are no suggestions here regarding punishment. Excessive digging is a symptom of a larger problem. Digging is the dog's way of releasing pent up energy, boredom, and frustration. Alleviate your dog's boredom by signing her up for fun obedience classes or by taking a class to teach your dog tricks or agility, and be sure to regularly provide stimulating toys that he doesn't see every day. Be creative in providing lots of stimulating activities for your dog and you will be rewarded with a calm, more content family pet and a lot fewer holes in your backyard.

CHAPTER 19
Lunging and On-Leash Aggression

Dog aggression sometimes gets its start from inappropriate leash manners in a young dog. Adult dogs find it rude when an adolescent dog jumps on them or gets in their space uninvited. The human end of the leash often makes the problem worse by making the leash too short and not paying attention to what the dog is doing.

Leashes Can Cause Aggressive Behavior

When dogs are off leash and encounter other dogs or stimuli, they are free to get away, display a "don't bother me" attitude, or simply invite the other dog to play. Dogs on leash cannot show these same emotions, and feel more cornered and threatened. Leashes and the owners who hold them can make it impossible for dogs to give the appropriate signals to each other and tend to get in the way of communicating rather than helping the dogs get along. Dog owners who fear their dog's reaction to other dogs often don't help matters because they tense up and tighten the leash, signaling to the dog that trouble lies ahead.

Owner Manners

People with on-leash dogs tend to approach each other head-on, whereas dogs normally approach one another in a curved half circle. Approaching head-to-head is a combative signal that says you mean business and may want to fight. Your dog may recognize another dog's rank and lower himself ever so slightly to signal to the other dog that he means no harm. As a human, however, you pull yourself and the leash upright when you see the other dog coming. Pulling up on the leash changes your dog's body posture into a more threatening stance, causing the other dog to react and your dog to become defensive. The higher-ranking dog is taken by surprise and attacks your dog for changing his mind and posturing the wrong message at the last moment. No wonder it is difficult for on-leash dogs to get along!

QUESTIONS?

What should I do when my dog greets another dog *on* leash?
It is crucial to keep a loose leash when allowing your dog to greet another dog on leash. Always ask first to make sure the other dog is normally friendly and let the dogs approach each other from the side rather than the front.

The person holding the leash is often the one responsible for the greeting going badly, as he or she inadvertently pulls the dog into a more dominant posture, which sends exactly the wrong message to the other dog. The source of the problem comes down to poor leash manners on the dog's part and not enough control on the owner's part.

Dog Manners

Dogs that, in play, launch themselves at other on-leash dogs are also sending the wrong message. Jumping on other dogs that are trapped on leash and can't get away is rude and bad dog manners. Dogs that do this are often corrected sharply by other dogs, and their owners often mistake this for true aggression. If this scenario is repeated enough, the friendly dog starts to learn to be defensive and the beginnings of leash aggression result. The reality here is that the jumping dog has poor leash manners and broke the cardinal rule: no jumping on an adult dog.

 SSENTIALS

Leash manners for well-socialized dogs include not pulling or lunging around other dogs, sitting when greeting another dog and owner, and only going to other dogs with permission.

No on-leash dog should have to put up with another dog jumping on him, even in play. It is important as the owner of your dog to make sure that you have appropriate control of your dog around other dogs. The more well trained your dog is the better accepted he will be by other on-leash dogs, and people as well. Too many bad experiences will make the dog wary of approaching other dogs on leash and cause reflexive, defensive aggression.

The Leash

The best type of leash for walking an aggressive dog is a six-foot nylon or leather leash. A dog with lunging and aggression problems should not be on an extendable leash, nor should she ever be off leash around other dogs. A six-foot leash allows you to control your dog and keep her close to you. The way you hold the leash is important to your dog's progress as well. In general it is best to hold it with two hands, one hand through the loop end and the other about halfway down the length. This allows your dog a little slack but not so much that she can lunge ahead of you without you being able to easily prevent it. Holding the leash too tightly so that your dog has barely enough room to move is not recommended. Don't force your dog to walk right next to you; let her have a little slack. The slacker the leash is (without letting her get too far ahead of you), the less confined and cornered she will feel when she sees another dog. When the leash is attached to a Gentle Leader Headcollar, remember that it is self-correcting and does not require you to jerk or pull. If your dog tries to lunge, the action will naturally pull her head to the ground. Before your dog lunges, you should try to get her attention back on you and move in the opposite direction. Make sure you are prepared not only to move away from the other dog, but to click and treat your dog for moving with you. Throwing the reward on the ground is also a good idea, because it may be a little more interesting for your dog, giving you the time you need to get her under control while the other dog goes on its way.

The way you hold the leash is an important part of successful dog interactions. The looser the leash, the better able your dog is to show other dogs that he means no harm. Maintaining slack in the leash will enable your dog to discriminate friendly dogs from not so friendly ones. Many behavior problems started with a leash that was too tight and a dog with no leash manners.

Leash Manners

For dogs with good social skills that get into trouble when on leash, take some simple steps to help improve on-leash manners. First of all, you need to use the right equipment. There are lots of products on the market today that help you to control your dog's pulling. The problem with these devices is that they fool you into thinking your dog knows not to pull on his leash, but as soon as the device is removed the dog goes back to pulling. The important thing to keep in mind is that all training collars and devices are just that, devices. They facilitate training; they do not replace it. Regardless of what piece of training equipment you use, you must click and treat your dog for not pulling and eventually label it and wean the dog off the treats, clicker, and the collar.

Golden Retriever saying she's "sorry"

The mistake most people make is that they put training collars on dogs that don't know not to pull and they expect the dogs to somehow magically figure out what they want them to do. If you don't reward your dog for the right behavior, you will not get the right behavior. When using a training collar, you must reward the dog for walking with you, or the dog will have no idea what is expected of him. The way the training collar works is that when the dog pulls, the handler jerks and releases the leash to make pulling an unpleasant choice. The dog is supposed to stop pulling (at least for a second). The dog must then be rewarded when it stops pulling or no real learning will occur.

Most dogs that are not rewarded for the appropriate behavior end up thinking the exercise is "run to the end of the leash, your owner gives you a yank, go back to her side, and run to the end of the leash again." Not all dogs will respond this way, however. Some very sensitive dogs will fall apart the first time they are corrected and never try to pull again, but they are doing so out of fear, not because they have learned that you want them next to you. Sensitive dogs should probably not wear a training collar in the first place since they learn quickly through much more gentle methods.

The head halter (see Chapter 15) works very well while training your dog not to pull. The leash clip is under the dog's chin, so there is no constriction of the windpipe when the dog pulls. These collars are also self-correcting. When the dog pulls forward, the head is forced down, effectively stopping the dog from moving forward. This means that there is no need to jerk on the leash or correct your dog; in fact, doing so may damage his neck. The head halter teaches a dog not to pull by operating on several principles:

1. A dog that pulls while wearing a head halter ends up with her nose to the ground and can not walk forward until she puts slack in the leash.
2. Since the halter fits over the dog's neck and muzzle, it gives the handler complete control over the dog's head.
3. If you control where the head goes, the body must follow.
4. The way the collar fits (over the back of the neck and over the top of the muzzle) mimics what a mother dog does when she disciplines her pups.
5. Because the owner now has complete control, many dogs learn to trust their handlers and pay more attention to them.

The head halter is a must for teaching on-leash manners. When used correctly, this device will not only prevent lunging, but also lower the dog's head and body carriage, which will make him less likely to provoke other dogs. The simple fact that you now control the dog's head is enough to prevent future repetitions of the problem.

Reward the Right Behavior

Teach your dog to be polite on leash around other dogs by clicking and treating him for approaching dogs sideways instead of head-on, for turning his head away instead of staring, and for offering a play Bow instead of jumping on the other dog. The play Bow (see Chapter 6), a natural behavior in which the dog puts its chest and belly close to the ground and the fanny in the air, is a behavior you can put on cue so that you can ask your dog to Bow when greeting another dog.

A dog that isn't getting enough exercise is sure to be obnoxious on leash. His built-up energy has to come out somehow and will manifest itself in lunging, leaping, and frantic on-leash behavior. If this describes your dog, provide more exercise and outlets for his pent-up energy and exuberance for life.

Remember that when teaching a dog to heel on leash, the most important point is to not follow a dog that is pulling. When your dog pulls and you follow, you are reinforcing your dog for pulling to get where he wants to go. If your dog is a few years old he probably already has a substantial bank account for pulling and lunging, and you will have some training to do if you are going to compete with that. The first step is to make lots of turns so that you are always in the lead and your dog has to closely watch you to see where you are going to end up next. Changing direction and clicking and treating your dog for catching up is the key to teaching your dog that being next to you is better than pulling or lagging behind. With lots of repetition and changes in variables and distractions, your dog will start to understand that walking on leash means walking next to you, not yanking you down the street.

Teach Your Dog to Leave It

Leave It means that the dog stops and looks back at her handler. This definition will help you in many situations, from your dog chasing a cat or squirrel across a busy street to lunging at another dog or person. Leave It means "stop what you are doing or thinking about doing and look in my direction." Once your dog is looking at you, you have a much greater chance of getting her to respond to your directions to Heel, Come, Lie Down, or whatever. Teaching your dog to Leave It is probably the most important thing your dog must learn if she is going to be safe to walk in public places. The faster and more reliable response to this behavior, the better your control will be.

For dogs that lack social skills, training your dog to Leave It will be your best management tool. The longer the duration of looking at you that your dog can master, the better able you will be to control him around other dogs and people. Leave It is an invaluable command for dogs that lunge at other dogs on leash. When teaching Leave It, it is important to catch the dog before he starts to lunge and bark. Once the dog is barking and lunging he is no longer in learning mode, and no amount of yelling or corrections will get him there. You must beat him to this highly charged emotional state by interrupting him before he really notices the other dog and then reversing direction so that he moves with you. Click and treat your dog for moving away from the other dog and going with you. One way to increase your dog's enthusiasm for turning away is to throw a whole handful of treats in the grass so that he has to hunt them up. The time it takes for him to do this will give the other dog and owner time to go by you. When he's finished, you can continue on your walk.

Because following you and leaving the distraction is a new pattern of behavior, you'll have to practice it over and over until your dog does it almost automatically. With enough repetition he may even start to offer the behavior on his own. If your timing is off, and you don't turn him in time, he will explode into a frenzy of barking. There is nothing you can do at this point except to just get through it and try again the next time. By not yelling at or correcting the dog you will at least not be reinforcing the undesirable behavior.

Here are the steps to teaching your dog to leave another dog:

1. Use familiar dogs at first so that you can completely control your training session and the dogs. Have your helper and "distraction dog" start on the opposite side of the street at first.
2. Make sure you interrupt your dog when he's thinking about lunging or barking. Interrupt him by saying his name and then turning 180 degrees in the opposite direction. Click and treat him for turning with you.
3. If your dog doesn't turn with you, it means that you are too close to the distraction dog; move away from the other dog by a couple of more feet and try again.
4. Throw a whole handful of goodies for him to clean up after you click so that you make it well worth his while to pay attention to you.
5. Once your dog is ignoring the other dog and turning with you easily, shorten the distance by having the dog approach on the same side of the street and repeat from the start.
6. Build up to being able to have the distraction dog pass within several feet with no reaction from your dog.
7. Change the distractions by using different dogs and changing where you practice until your dog can ignore any dog anywhere.

ESSENTIALS

For training purposes, the "distraction dog" should be a completely reliable well-socialized adult dog that will not react to the aggressive dog in anyway. It will also help to have the distraction dog wear a head halter to help the aggressive dog perceive him as nonthreatening. Vary the scenarios until your dog is eagerly looking to you when she sees other dogs.

Set Reasonable Goals

Dogs with little or no social skills are never going to be totally friendly or trustworthy with other dogs. There is no such thing as resocializing an adult dog with no experience with other dogs. Doing so would be dangerous and most likely end in injury to dogs or the humans that interfered. The best that can be done with dogs like this is to set a reasonable goal. Your goal might be to have your dog like other dogs, but a more reasonable goal might be to have her respond immediately to your command to Leave It.

Teaching your dog appropriate leash manners of not lunging or barking and turning her head away from other dogs rather than staring them down will mean you can take her more places and be able to control her. Acknowledge that though you would like your dog to get along with other dogs, your dog is perfectly content to not have any contact with them. Don't force your own desire for your dog to have friends on your best pal; she may feel she has as many friends as she needs, and no amount of pushing on your part will change that. Respect what your dog is trying to tell you and keep her safe around other dogs.

If you have a young puppy, let him meet and play with as many different kinds of puppies and adult dogs as you can. The window for socializing a dog to other dogs is short, between seven and eighteen weeks. As the window closes, your dog is less open to new experiences and less likely to be social with other dogs.

Make the Commitment

The worst thing you can do with this type of problem is to be in a rush. Your dog did not get this way overnight and no one thing you do is going to magically change your dog's opinion of other dogs. This process of teaching appropriate manners to a dog with no social experience around dogs is time consuming. You must be totally committed to helping improve your dogs behavior in order to even put a dent in the problem. A halfhearted attempt to change your dog's behavior will not help you reach your goal. In order to make progress you will have to do hundreds of repetitions of Leave It and put lots of time into practicing keeping the leash loose. This is a long-term program; don't expect miracles overnight. As with anything in life, you get out of it what you put into it. If you practice diligently and set reasonable goals you will eventually be rewarded by a more enjoyable walking companion.

Lack of Socialization

So far, you've read about dogs with fairly good social skills but with bad leash manners. What about dogs that have not been socialized with other dogs? Dogs that lack social experience are a more serious problem than dogs with bad leash manners. The reason for this is simple: Dogs with social skills know that not all dogs are going to attack them and have had good experiences with other dogs. Dogs that have not been socialized with other dogs have nothing to go on, and every dog they see, friendly or not, is perceived as a threat. Dogs that have no canine social skills are not, and never will be, socially normal.

Socializing a dog to other dogs must happen when the dog is a puppy between eight and eighteen weeks of age. If the puppy is not around other pups and adult dogs at this age it will never be socially normal with other dogs. Socialization is like training, however, and must be fostered and maintained throughout the animal's entire life; if dogs don't get to practice their social skills, they lose them. Dogs need to play with others of their own kind to learn the ins and outs of acceptable behavior and appropriate body language. Without these experiences they begin to act suspiciously and aggressively toward other dogs. Most people notice this problem is even worse on leash because the dog feels trapped and can't escape.

The Bar Is Open Technique

Classical conditioning can be a very powerful tool in getting faster and more reliable results in your training program. The Bar Is Open, the Bar Is Closed technique uses the principles of classical conditioning to change the way your dog feels about other dogs on leash. Classical conditioning deals with associations (see Chapter 13). The presence of other dogs means that the bar is open and all kinds of good things happen, including affection, attention, and treats, regardless of the dog's behavior. (He can be lunging or barking hysterically and you continue to drop treats like it is Christmas). When the other dog disappears, so do the treats and games and attention; in fact, the handler gives the dog the outright cold shoulder.

E ALERT

When using classical conditioning to change your dog's behavior, you'll want to be sure you keep your distance so that the other dogs can't come right up to you. Be sure your dog is on leash and at enough of a distance so as to give her every opportunity for success.

Classical conditioning tries to change the way the dog feels about having other dogs around by associating other dogs with good things. The drawback of this technique is that it takes the animal time to realize the association between the good stuff and the offending presence of another dog. The way to use this technique effectively is to practice frequently so as to give your dog an increasingly big bank account for liking the sight of other dogs. Eventually your dog will like having other dogs around because it means that he is going to have access to all the things he loves.

Here's how it works in real life:

- Choose a spot where other dogs are likely to pass by and bring all of your very best reinforcements. This can range from cheese, liver, and hot dogs, to tennis balls, tug toys, and squeaky toys.
- When other dogs are within sight, regardless of your dog's behavior, the bar is open. You bounce the ball, throw it, roll it, and shower your dog with treats, toys, and attention. As soon as the dog is out of sight, the bar is closed. You put your goodies away, step on the leash, and ignore your dog completely for at least a full two minutes.
- When another dog comes by, you again open the bar; when it disappears, the bar is closed.

- After repeating this over and over again your dog is going to learn a new reaction to other dogs. He is going to learn that when other dogs are present, good things happen, and when they go the fun is over.

Lunging and on-leash aggression is a fairly serious behavior problem, one that requires lots of consistent practice in order to change it. It is not a behavior that will go away with just a little training, and it is one that needs to be constantly maintained. Dogs revert back to old habits if you don't consistently reinforce the right behaviors. Consider this behavior problem one that needs constant maintenance to ensure that the dog adopts the new behavior of turning away as a habit.

Remember that bad habits are hard to get rid of because they are comfortable (think of eating the wrong foods, or smoking). If a new behavior is going to replace an old one, there must be some planning involved and time set aside for practice. Keep in mind that as with any old habit, there will be regression and mistakes. Plan for them so that you're ready to get back on track and so that they don't totally derail you. With time, patience, love, and training you can make any dog a better companion.

CHAPTER 20

Canine Social Skills

D ogs are social animals that learn to interact and get along with each other by playing together from a very young age. The best way for them to learn how to get along is for them to play with lots of other dogs during the most impressionable time in their lives, the first eight to eighteen weeks of age.

Socialization Versus Training

Training a dog the basics of Sit, Stay, and Come can be accomplished at any age, but the ideal time to socialize your dog to other dogs, people, and new experiences is between the ages of eight to eighteen weeks. Once a puppy is eighteen weeks, she is less open to new experiences and she begins to gravitate toward the familiar rather than explore the new. You must of course continue to give your dog social experiences beyond the age of eighteen weeks, but if you don't start before then you are sentencing your dog to a life of fearful and suspicious reactions to other dogs, new experiences, and people.

Socializing a dog is an investment of time and energy and should include not only experiences with other dogs but with people of all shapes and sizes and new experiences as well. It isn't good enough to just show up in public; careful planning is required to make sure your dog has positive experiences that will benefit her for a lifetime. Giving your dog a varied experience of life will teach her from an early age to cope with sounds, sights, smells, new people, and a variety of breeds and mixed breeds of dogs. By making an effort to socialize your dog, you are increasing your dog's ability to learn how to act around people and other dogs, and you are giving her the best chance of becoming an adult dog that is well mannered and friendly. A good solid social experience will benefit her for a lifetime.

ESSENTIALS

Although it's imperative to begin socialization around the first month of a puppy's life, it's also important to keep at it to keep the dog open to new experiences. A dog that consistently encounters new things, places, and people will remain well socialized.

Dogs have a critical socialization window during which time they should meet at least a hundred people and a hundred other dogs and puppies. The window opens sometime around the second week of life when the puppies first open their eyes, and the window starts to close around the eighteenth week. This doesn't mean that socialization stops there. It must continue beyond this point, but it means that your puppy is most impressionable at this age and can accept new experiences more easily than an older dog. The more positive experiences with people and other dogs that your puppy has during this time, the more willing she will be to accept and get along with people and dogs for the rest of her life. You can make or break a dog's potential by offering the right socialization at the right time.

Socialization is not the same for every dog. There are as many personality types among dogs as there are among people: some are outgoing, some are shy, some are overbearing, some are vocal, some are physical, and so on. A puppy's play style will often determine what types of puppies he should play with in order to learn the right ways to get along with other dogs.

Socializing Your Dog to Other Dogs

Socialization to other dogs is perhaps the most overlooked aspect of a dog's social experience. The more dogs and puppies a young dog meets, the better able he will be to get along with any dog, anywhere. Not supplying your dog with the skills with which to get along with other dogs may well be a form of abuse and neglect. Most of the private training that owners seek involves dogs that are aggressive with other dogs. When a dog has enough social experience with other dogs during his critical window of socialization, he learns how to get along with dogs. Without the right kind of social experience however, behavior problems develop.

Pay Attention to Play Styles

Rowdy puppies should not be allowed to play rough for long periods of time. By having these types of dogs play with other dogs of varying personality types—ranging from shy puppies to outgoing puppies, adolescent and adult dogs (who are not as tolerant of rude puppy antics)—you have the best chance of teaching the boisterous puppy how to adjust his play style to any dog, shy or not. Letting a rowdy puppy play only with other rowdy puppies is asking for trouble. This pup will grow up to be obnoxious around other dogs and will not be well liked. Obnoxious adult dogs are not tolerated well by other adult dogs because they have no manners. They jump, roughhouse, and mouth too roughly, and as a result they are often overcorrected by other dogs. The rowdy adult dog is often the dog that all the other dogs pile upon because all the dogs that are present feel he needs to be taught a lesson. The rowdy pup needs lots of social experience: consider doggie day care to help him meet all kinds of dogs that will teach him the rules of getting along with the group.

ESSENTIALS

To preserve your dog's healthy social development, monitor her playmates so that she's not playing too rough for too long a period of time. Some rough play is okay, but too much will teach your puppy that being out of control is the way to play. Vary your dog's experience by going new places and meeting lots of different dogs.

Playful puppies are middle-of-the-road types; they can play rough with the rowdy dog or tone it down to play with the shyer dogs. They are born peacemakers and party dogs. These pups can be with any type of dog and have a great experience. At our doggie day care we call this type of dog a "cheerleader." This is the dog that will invite any dog to play and be the most easygoing dog in the group. Owners of this type of pup need to be careful that their puppies don't get too overwhelmed by more enthusiastic dogs. Don't be afraid to initiate little breaks in the action and let your dog cool down a bit before sending her back in for more fun.

Wallflowers

Unlike rowdy or energetic pups, shy dogs would wilt in a group of rowdy pups, learning to be fearful and defensive instead of playful. These dogs should spend huge amounts of time with playful pups that invite them to play but are not too boisterous. Playful puppies invite shy dogs to interact by play bowing, barking (not excessively), and kissing the other puppy. The playful puppy will continue to invite the shy pup to play until eventually he wears him down. A shy puppy needs triple the amount of social experience as the average dog, but it needs to be carefully calculated so as not to overwhelm him. If you own a shy puppy, enroll it in a well-organized puppy kindergarten, as well as considering a carefully selected doggie day care. Be sure the day care folks know how to socialize a shy dog and provide downtime via a nap in a crate or separate room several times throughout the day.

Lab Mix targets a hand with his nose

Socialization to People

The easiest part of socializing a puppy simply involves showing up in public with a clicker and treats to make sure all new experiences are fun and rewarding. Bring plenty of delicious treats and a toy to keep the puppy's mouthing under control. Go to parks and pet stores, or visit the groomer or the neighbors. Take your puppy as many new places as possible; let him hear, see, and experience the world. Be careful how you introduce your puppy to these new experiences, though. If she seems afraid or unsure of herself, go slowly. Try backing off a bit, using your best treats and happy voice to encourage your puppy to investigate.

Never force an unwilling puppy to investigate something it's terrified of; a bad experience can set you back weeks. Building confidence is a slow process, which works best if you provide your puppy with proof that the world is a safe and interesting place.

When a puppy is fearful of new people and strange things, the best way to help build your puppy's confidence is to let him take his time warming up and reward his bravery. A dog can't learn anything when it is afraid—so don't force him. By working at your dog's comfort level you are putting money in the bank for building confidence. Keep the experience fun, upbeat, and varied, and your puppy will develop into a confident adult dog.

Start Early

The more early intervention you can provide, the easier it will be for your pup to learn to cope with new experiences. By having some tricks up your sleeve you will have more options in helping your puppy to have good experiences regardless of the circumstances.

1. Teach your pup how to target your hand (see Chapter 4) and use this to introduce new people and objects.
2. Work at your pup's comfort level with the goal being to gradually get him closer.
3. Go at least two new places each week.
4. Continue to help your dog have good experiences despite the extra effort.
5. Get out there—there is harm in waiting.

6. Continue past sixteen to eighteen weeks of age, but start sooner if possible.
7. Enlist the help of family and friends.
8. Break scary new experiences into small attainable goals.
9. Avoid moving too fast; if you overwhelm your pup, don't be afraid to quit and try again later.

Some Dogs Need More Social Experience

Depending on your dog's breed and personality she may need more social experience than the average dog. The working and herding breeds are notoriously more suspicious of new people and experiences. If you think about what these dogs do for work, it makes a lot of sense. Working and herding dogs are bred to notice what is different and react to it, which is what makes them so good at herding and guarding. No wonder they need double the amount of socialization than the average dog in order to differentiate between friend and foe. The more good experiences they have the better able they will be to accept new people and things as a normal part of their world.

What about Doggie Day Care?

Doggie day care facilities are popping up all over the place and provide dogs with nonstop canine fun. Active dogs enjoy wrestling and playing with other dogs, and they get lots of attention from the human staff. Day care a few times a week or everyday can make a huge difference in the hours you spend together at home and on the weekends. Most working people come home too tired to exercise an active dog for two hours. With doggie day care, however, that same owner could spend those two hours enjoying her dog in some other way.

Day care is a great way to give an active dog an outlet for all his energy, a shy dog an opportunity for new experiences, and a boisterous dog a chance to meet all kinds of dogs so as to learn how to adjust his play style to the dogs he's playing with. Following are some tips for searching for the right doggie day care.

- The dogs should have their own water bowls to prevent the spread of viruses.
- The dogs should be separated into groups according to age, personality, and play style, with no more than ten to fifteen dogs per group.
- An enhanced rest time via crates, separate mats, or runs should be part of the day. This ensures that active dogs learn self-control and shy or playful ones get a break from the other dogs.
- There should be one attendant for every ten dogs.
- Day care attendants should be adults who have been properly trained in normal (and abnormal) dog behavior, including how to safely break up a dogfight.
- A strong disinfectant and anti-viral solution should be used to clean up accidents.
- All dogs should be required to be vaccinated or titered, spayed or neutered.
- All dogs should be in good health and not have symptoms of vomiting or diarrhea, eye discharge or a cough.
- Dogs that are aggressive toward people or other dogs should not be allowed at day care for the safety of everyone.
- Go in person to meet the staff and see how they run their day and make sure the indoor and outdoor facilities are clean and secure.

The best candidates for day care are puppies and young adult dogs. If you are unable to get your dog out to lots of different places to play with other dogs, day care may be a great option for you.

QUESTIONS?

What is a _vaccine titer_?
A vaccine titer is a blood test performed on a vaccinated dog to determine its level of immunity to a given disease. In general, if a titer is positive, the animal has immunity to that particular disease. If the animal does not have a positive titer, consult your veterinarian before having your pet revaccinated.

Most doggie day care facilities will interview you and your dog, which gives you the opportunity to see the facility and ask questions. Go with a checklist and be sure you are comfortable with the style of the day care facility before leaving your dog there. Interview at several places and talk to other dog owners before you make your decision.

Abused or Unsocialized?

Many dog owners mistakenly assume that their adopted or rescued dog was abused because they are shy or aggressive around new people or dogs. These dogs tend to cower and shake or act aggressive, lunging and barking. Often, the reality is that the dog has not been socialized to people, dogs, and new experiences, and reacts aggressively or shyly out of fear and lack of confidence.

The best way to help a dog that behaves in this manner is to train her and build her confidence around new people, dogs, and experiences. Making excuses for shy or aggressive dogs or trying to cuddle and comfort them will not fix the problem, and it could make it worse. Remedial socialization (socializing a dog after the optimum age of eight to eighteen weeks) is time consuming and fraught with regression and frustration but ultimately well worth the effort. Some socialization tips for shy or aggressive dogs include:

1. Teach your dog how to target your hand and extend it to people and objects.
2. Build confidence slowly by taking your time and allowing for regression.
3. Increase the distance by backing away from the person or object until the dog is comfortable.
4. If you are working with new people, have them be as neutral as possible. Have them turn to the side, make no direct eye contact with the dog, and let it be the dog's idea to go to them.
5. Use the best treats; you want to associate new experiences with the things the dog really likes.

Choose Your Dog's Playmates Carefully

Don't wait until your dog is fully vaccinated to begin socializing it, but do carefully choose the dogs it meets and plays with. It isn't a good idea to take a pup that is between eight and twelve weeks old to the local park and let it meet just any old dog or eat other dogs' feces. Enroll your young dog in a well-organized puppy kindergarten class before it is sixteen weeks old and make sure that all the puppies attending the class have been started on their vaccinations.

FACTS

A varied social experience is an insurance policy against bad experiences that might alter a dog's future behavior. Because they will have a lot of experience to draw upon, they will be able to go back to enjoying the experience of being with other dogs.

Most puppies get their last series of shots at sixteen weeks of age, but if you wait until your dog is that old to get him around other dogs, you will probably find that he is shy and defensive and not as outgoing and adventurous as he may have been at an earlier age. This is a sign that the socialization window is closing and you need to increase and intensify his experience around other dogs. In short, if you wait to begin your dog's socialization until he is fully vaccinated, you will find you have to work harder at getting him to like being around other dogs. More dogs die every year from behavior problems resulting from a lack of socialization than dogs exposed to the more common viruses that we vaccinate against. So get out there and make sure every puppy you ever own from now on gets to meet lots of other dogs and people so he avoids becoming another statistic.

CHAPTER 21

Canine Public Relations

Everywhere you look there are restrictions on dogs. The No Dogs Allowed policy has been adopted by parks, hotels, and beaches across the nation. Things are changing slowly, however, due to an enormous education effort aimed at teaching dog owners how to be more responsible for their dogs, and considerate of their non-dog-owning neighbors.

Be a Goodwill Ambassador

Though you may consider your pet your child, it's important to remember that not everyone shares your enthusiasm. People who don't like dogs often have experience with inconsiderate and irresponsible dog owners. Such folks own dogs that bark all day and night, or early in the morning, they leave unscooped poop on lawns or sidewalks, they let their dog run off leash through their neighbor's yards, and allow their dogs to be out of control. Being a goodwill ambassador for dogs means taking care not to allow your dog to intrude on someone else's space uninvited. Showing responsibility by example is the greatest way to ensure more people can take dogs more places.

FACTS

Leash laws exist in most residential communities and are often only enforced when someone complains to the local dog officer. Fines vary from city to city, but repeat offenses are not looked kindly upon. Be considerate of your neighbors and be sure your dog does not run loose in the neighborhood.

Basic Dog-Walking Manners

Taking your dog for a walk through your neighborhood or the local park can be a wonderfully relaxing way to enjoy a beautiful day, but you should observe some basic good dog owner's etiquette so that everyone can enjoy the great outdoors. Be a responsible dog owner:

- Walk your dog on a leash in your neighborhood and don't allow him to urinate or mark people's property, including trees, bushes, and posts, etc.
- Take care to train your dog a Leave It command with regard to leg lifting, to cut short his effort to claim your neighbor's property as his own.
- When you allow your dog off-leash freedom, be sure she has a reliable Leave It and Come. A dog that lacks training in these areas does not belong off leash.

- If your dog is aggressive toward people or dogs, he should never be off leash in public places.
- Before you release your dog to be leash free, look around you and be sure she won't be disturbing other people who may be hiking or picnicking in the park.
- Don't allow your dog to jump on people even if he's friendly; put your foot on the leash to prevent jumping and teach him to Sit instead.
- Always carry a few bags with you and clean up after your dog poops.
- Supervise your dog closely around other dogs or children to make sure no one is getting overly exuberant.

ALERT

Besides annoying your neighbors, loose dogs often eat things they shouldn't, dig up other people's lawns, and get hit by cars. Keeping your dog safely at home will mean he gets to live out his life in a fun, safe environment provided by someone who loves him and wants him to live to a ripe old age.

Whether you are walking in your neighborhood, taking your dog to the local park for a romp, or hiking in the woods, paying attention to basic good-dog-owner etiquette will ensure that others after you will be able to enjoy their dogs in the same places. Dog owners who are careful to manage their dog's behavior in public pass on a lasting image to the people around them that dogs deserve access to public places. If you are tired of public places banning dogs, this is one small way to change the image the public has of out-of-control dogs running amok and creating havoc.

"Curb Your Dog"

There is no excuse for not picking up after your dog. Carry bags with you every time you are out with your dog, and scoop regardless if anyone is looking or not! No one, even the craziest dog lover, likes stepping in poop. There are lots of new products on the market today that make the scooping job easy. You can use any type of plastic bag, but the kind that reclose are cheap and easy and have the added benefit of sealing in the odor. Just turn the bag inside out, scoop the pile, carefully, turn the bag right-side out, and zip.

ESSENTIALS

There are many different poop bag holders available. Some attach to the leash and not only carry spare bags, but have a spot for your keys and change as well. Cleaning up after your dog announces to your neighbors that you are a responsible dog owner and that you care about how your pet affects others.

Nuisance Barkers

If your dog is a barker, don't leave it outside to practice barking. If there is one thing that sends people over the edge, it's an incessantly barking dog. Dogs are pack animals that want to be with their families; they don't like to be left out, and will express frustration and boredom through persistent barking. If you have a barking problem with your dog you owe it to yourself, your dog, and your neighbors to address it and train your dog not to bark. Be considerate of your neighbors: don't leave your dog outside in the early morning or late at night if you know she will bark at the slightest noise. Nothing makes neighbors angrier than a dog that wakes them up early in the morning or keeps them from falling asleep at night.

Review the many ways to train your dog to stop barking (see Chapter 12), and become familiar with the nitty-gritty on why most dogs bark and how best to teach them not to. Here are some tips for curbing barking behavior:

- **Provide plenty of exercise.** One to two hours a day of running, swimming, playing with other dogs, etc., is essential. Consider a doggie day care program in your area.
- **Block the view.** Use shrubs, a stockade fence, or some other barrier so your dog cannot see who's passing through.

- **Provide mental stimulation.** Stuff Kong toys with peanut butter and dog food, and let your dog get all his meals out of his toys.
- **Meet your dog's needs.** Spend time with your dog and learn how to communicate with him. Enroll in a training class that uses fun, positive methods, like clicker training, that teach your dog how to think.
- **Avoid the "quick fix."** Resist the temptation to buy devices that claim to stop your dog from barking. They are quick fixes that either don't work or use too harsh a correction; train your dog instead.

Leaving a Dog in a Car

In addition to being responsible *for* their dogs, dog owners are also responsible *to* their dogs. Responsible dog owners do not leave their dogs in cars on days when the temperature is over 70 degrees, even with the windows down. Dogs can quickly succumb to heat stroke and die if left as little as ten minutes in an enclosed car on a warm day. Even with the air conditioning on, things can happen, like your car stalling or running out of gas. If you go out on a warm day, don't take a chance with your best friend's life: leave your dog at home where he is safe and comfortable.

The sun beating down on your car on a cool day can dramatically change the temperature in the car and make it uncomfortably hot. If you take your dog with you in the car, check on him frequently and make sure that he isn't getting too hot or uncomfortable.

If the temperature is not too hot or too cold and you do decide to take your dog with you, be sure she has adequate ventilation, but don't put the windows down so far that she could jump out and get lost or hit by a passing car. Be sure to remove her leash and training collar if she's wearing one so that it doesn't get caught on anything and strangle herself. Be sure if you do leave your dog in the car that it's not in full sun, even if the day is cool.

Reliable Recall and Other Owner Issues

In general your dog should only be off leash if he comes 100 percent of the time, has a good strong Leave It command, and does not jump on people he meets. With those three commands in place, you can reasonably control an off-leash dog. If you find that your dog is less than ideal in these areas, provide more training and practice before setting him loose on the public. Remember that everyone who meets your dog should come away with the feeling that dogs are sweet and gentle creatures that enhance the lives of their owners. If you're vigilant about your dog's manners, even non-dog-people will come to appreciate the value of dog ownership.

These are the basics of good off-leash manners:

- Teach reliable Come, Leave It, and Off commands.
- Teach your dog to Sit for petting instead of jumping.
- Teach your dog to Sit for thrown objects like balls and toys, and discourage jumping or mouthing for toys.
- Use a leash around groups of people, especially small children or people who are eating.
- Don't allow your dog to lift his leg on people's property, especially doorways, car tires, bushes, lawn statues, etc.
- Teach your dog to wait to be released to say hello to other dogs; not all dogs are friendly and want to say hello to your dog.

Even if your dog is extremely friendly with other dogs and you trust her off leash, be considerate of dogs that are on leash and don't allow your dog to greet another dog without the owner's permission. Many dogs are aggressive with other dogs, and responsible owners of this type of dog manage their dogs' behavior by keeping them leashed at all times. Respect other dogs' and owners' need for space, and call your dog away.

Aggression

Aggression among dogs is on the rise in large part because they lack early socialization. This may be due partly to a decrease in the number of open spaces where people can take their dogs to socialize. If your dog does not like other dogs, do not allow him off leash where there are other dogs. Avoid taking your dog places where he is certain to be defensive and afraid, making you both miserable. If your dog is aggressive toward people, walk and exercise him at a time of day when no one else is around in order to avoid confrontations. Be vigilant about not allowing people to interact with your dog if he has bitten people before. Enlist the help of a qualified professional dog trainer to help you with these problems and don't take chances.

Public Education

The more education exists about responsible dog ownership the more receptive the public will be toward dogs. Consider forming an association of responsible dog owners in your city and petitioning for public open spaces to exercise your dog. Stressing your role as a taxpayer who enjoys the companionship of your dog is essential to gaining access to public spaces. Using a little social peer pressure to get dog-owning neighbors and friends to comply with pooper-scooper laws, leash manners, and overall pet owner responsibility is a giant step toward the acceptance of dogs in public spaces.

FACTS

Cleaning up after your dog and respecting other people's property and space are ways that you can help educate the public about responsible dog ownership. Encouraging other dog owners to do the same is crucial to ensuring that dog lovers everywhere get to enjoy their dogs in public places.

The Best Canine Public Relations Option

Therapy dogs visit people in hospitals and nursing homes nationwide and make enormous differences in people's lives. Therapy dogs should be trained in obedience and in general have a sweet personality and love to be with people. There are several different organizations that certify dogs for this type of work. The Delta Society is the largest resource for this type of information (see Appendix A for contact information). Being a member of a therapy-dog organization will not only help provide you with insurance coverage, but more importantly, it will give you the benefit of belonging to an organization that supports and guides the use of animals in hospitals and nursing homes.

Two Welsh Terriers and an Airedale Terrier

The work of a therapy dog is varied. It may simply be a visit involving cuddling or petting, or something more complicated like a speech lesson or physical therapy session. Regardless of its intensity, a visit from a therapy dog can change the course of a patient's treatment. There are countless stories of people talking for the first time or reaching some elusive milestone because of the presence of a dog. Dogs lighten the mood and make the work of rehabilitation in therapy a little less grueling. In nursing homes across the country, dogs take long, lonely, endless days and make them something to look forward to. Dogs can truly make a difference in a patient's life and give them hope. Therapy dogs have been helping people cope with life for decades. A therapy dog is a dog whose pure intelligence, beauty, and love are put to the best use possible.

Improve Your Dog's Image

Large, dark-colored dogs often make some people take a step back. Why not teach a scary-looking dog a silly trick to lighten people up. When a stranger who is afraid of your German shepherd or pit bull sees your dog playing dead, who has time to be afraid? Can you picture a big black Great Dane saying its prayers or waving hello. Non-dog-lovers have often had a bad experience with a dog that has left them suspicious of dogs that look tough or are dark in color (maybe it's because they can't see their facial expressions). Help change their experience not only by making sure that your dog is well mannered, but also by teaching your dog a silly trick to perform that will make it a fun and memorable encounter.

ESSENTIALS

No matter how friendly you know your dog to be, keep in mind that not everyone feels the same way about dogs as you do. Respect people's fearfulness and keep your distance until they invite your dog to greet them. Children especially may be fearful and should never be forced to greet a dog they don't want to greet.

Dogs bring such joy to those around them when they are trained and cared for by the people who love them. By educating yourself and your dog, you are investing back into your enjoyment of your dog and the interactions she has with those around her. Spread the word, set the example, and show the world that owning a dog is an experience no one should miss.

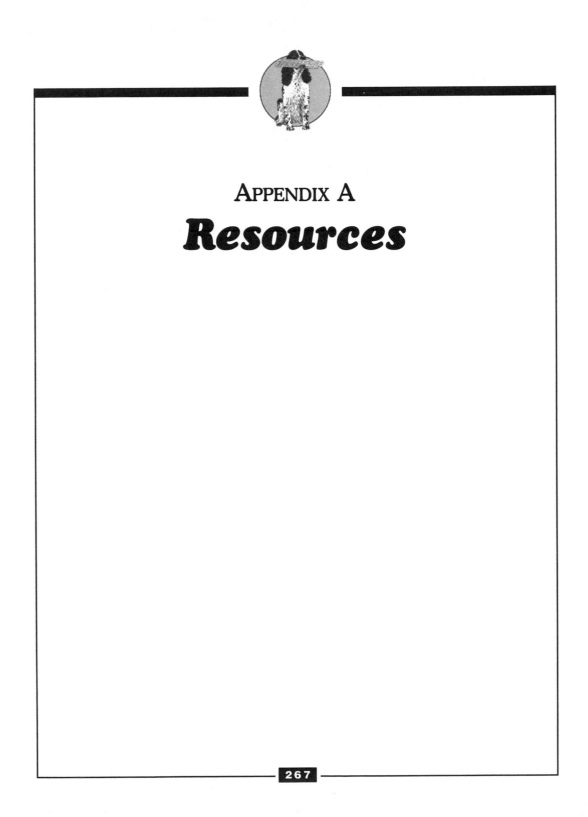

Appendix A

Resources

🐾 Books

Burch, Mary R. and Jon S. Bailey. *How Dogs Learn* (Hungry Minds, Inc., 1999).

Campbell, William E. *Behavior Problems in Dogs*, Third Revised Edition (BehaviorRx Systems, 1999).

Cantrell, Krista. *Catch Your Dog Doing Something Right: How to Train Any Dog in Five Minutes a Day* (Plume Publishers, 1998).

Donaldson, Jean. *The Culture Clash* (James and Kenneth Publishing, 1997).

Donaldson, Jean. *Dogs Are from Neptune* (Lasar Multimedia Productions, 1998).

Dunbar, Ian. *Dr. Dunbar's Good Little Dog Book* (James and Kenneth Publisher, 1992).

Dunbar, Ian. *How to Teach a New Dog Old Tricks* (James and Kenneth Publishing, 1998).

Owens, Paul. *The Dog Whisperer: A Compassionate, Nonviolent Approach to Dog Training* (Adams Media Corporation, 1999).

Pryor, Karen. *Don't Shoot the Dog: The New Art of Teaching and Training*, Revised Edition (Bantam Books, 1999).

Rugaas, Turid. *On Talking Terms with Dogs: Calming Signals* (Legacy By Mail, 1997).

Ryan, Terry. *The Toolbox for Remodeling Your Problem Dog* (Howell Book House, 1998).

Tellington-Jones, Linda. *Getting in Touch with Your Dog: A Gentle Approach to Influencing Health, Behavior, and Performance* (Trafalgar Square, 2001).

Wilkes, Gary. *A Behavior Sampler* (Sunshine Books, 1994).

🐾 Videos

Broitman, Virginia. *Bow Wow, Take 2* (Canine Training Systems, 1996).

Broitman, Virginia and Sherry Lippman. *Take a Bow Wow* (Canine Training Systems, 1996).

Jones, Deborah. *Click & Fetch* (Canine Training Systems, 1999).

Pryor, Karen. *Clicker Magic! The Art of Clicker Training* (Sunshine Books, 1997).

Pryor, Karen. *Puppy Love* (Sunshine Books, 1999).

Rugaas, Turid. *Calming Signals: What Your Dog Tells You* (Legacy By Mail, 2001).

Wilkes, Gary. *Click! & Treat Training Kit* (Click! & Treat Products, 1996).

Wilkes, Gary. *The Doggie Repair Kit* (Click! & Treat Products, 1996).

Organizations

The Association of Pet Dog Trainers (APDT)
Phone: 800-738-3647
Web site: *www.apdt.com*

Search the database for a list of trainers in your area.

Delta Society
Phone: 425-226-7357
Web site: *www.deltasociety.org*
E-mail: *info@deltasociety.org*

Therapy Dogs International
E-mail: *tdi@gti.net*

Whole-Dog Journal.com
Phone: 800-829-9165
Web site: *www.whole-dog-journal.com*

A monthly guide to natural dog care and training.

Web Sites

Association of Pet Dog Trainers (APDT)
www.apdt.com

Canine University®
www.canineuniversity.com

DogWise
www.dogwise.com

Note: This site sells all of the books and videos included in the book and video resources.

Karen Pryor's Web site
www.dontshootthedog.com

William Campbell's Web site
www.webtrail.com/petbehavior/index.html

APPENDIX B
Bibliography

Abrantes, Roger. *Dog Language: An Encyclopedia of Canine Behavior.* (Naperville, IL: Wakan Tanka Publishers, 1997).

Benjamin, Carol. *Dog Problems.* (New York, NY: Hungry Minds, Inc., 1989).

Campbell, William E. *Owner's Guide to Better Behavior in Dogs.* (Loveland, CO: Alpine Publishers, 1989).

Campbell, William E. *Behavior Problems in Dogs*, Third Revised Edition. (Grants Pass, OR: BehavioRx Systems, 1999).

Cantrell, Krista. *Catch Your Dog Doing Something Right: How to Train Any Dog in Five Minutes a Day.* (New York, NY: Plume Publishers, 1998).

Evans, Job Michael. *Training and Explaining: How to Be the Dog Trainer You Want to Be.* (New York, NY: Hungry Minds, Inc., 1995).

Fox, Dr. Michael W. *Understanding Your Dog.* (New York, NY: St. Martin's Press, 1972).

Milani, D.V.M., Myrna. *The Body Language and Emotions of Dogs.* (New York, NY; William Morrow and Company, 1986).

Milani, D.V.M., Myrna. *DogSmart.* (Chicago, IL: Contemporary Publishing, 1997).

Donaldson, Jean. *The Culture Clash.* (Berkeley, CA: James and Kenneth Publishers, 1997).

Donaldson, Jean. *Dogs Are from Neptune.* (Montreal, Quebec: Lasar Multimedia Productions, 1998).

Dunbar, Dr. Ian. *Dog Behavior.* (Neptune, NJ: TFH, 1979).

Dunbar, Dr. Ian. *How to Teach a New Dog Old Tricks.* (Berkeley, CA, James and Kenneth Publishers, 1998).

Owens, Paul. *The Dog Whisperer: A Compassionate, Nonviolent Approach to Dog Training.* (Avon, MA: Adams Media Corporation, 1999).

Pryor, Karen. *Karen Pryor on Behavior: Essays and Research.* (North Bend, WA: Sunshine Books, 1994).

Pryor, Karen. *Don't Shoot the Dog: The New Art of Teaching and Training*, Revised Edition. (New York, NY: Bantam Books, 1999).

Reid, Ph.D., Pamela. *Excel-Erated Learning: Explaining in Plain English How Dogs Learn and How Best to Teach Them.* (Oakland, CA: James and Kenneth Publishers, 1996).

Rugaas, Turid. *On Talking Terms with Dogs: Calming Signals.* (Carlsborg, WA: Legacy By Mail, 1997).

Ryan, Terry. *The Toolbox for Remodeling Your Problem Dog.* (New York, NY: Howell Book House, 1998).

Schwartz, Charlotte. *The Howell Book of Puppy Raising.* (New York, NY: Hungry Minds, Inc., 1987).

Scott, John Paul and John L. Fuller. *Genetics and the Social Behavior of the Dog.* (Chicago, IL: University of Chicago Press, 1965).

Wilkes, Gary. *A Behavior Sampler.* (North Bend, WA: Sunshine Books, 1994).

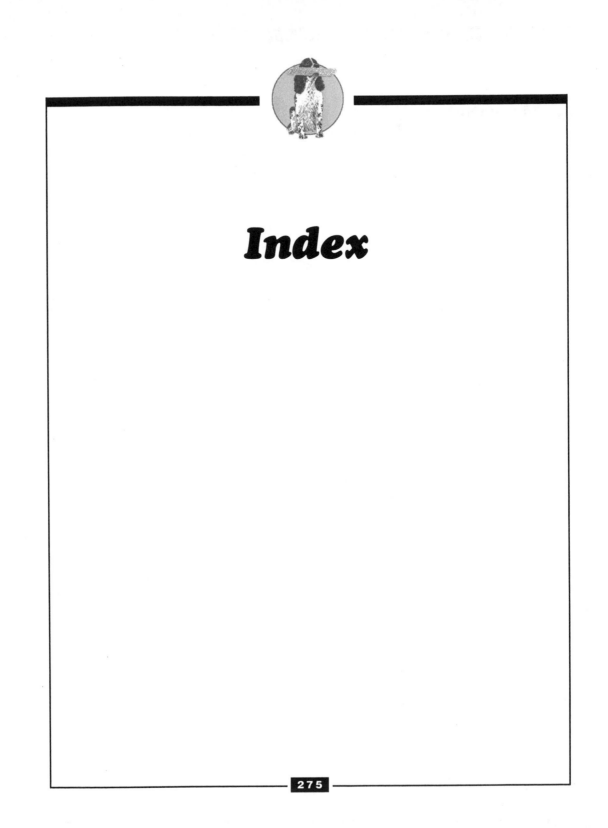

Index

F

fearful dogs, 161–173

    alternative strategies for, 172–173

    breeding and, 164–165

    classical conditioning for, 169–170

    heeling and, 197

    learning and, 131

    socialization and, 165–166, 252

    special needs of, 161–162

    systematic desensitization for, 170–171

    targeting and, 163–164, 168–169

    training plan for, 166–169

    tricks for, 144–145

    veterinary behaviorists and, 171–172

feet

    injuries to, 196

    safety and, 21

fence

    digging under, 229

    invisible, 213

fetching, 22, 89

Find It command, 104

Find My Car Keys Please trick, 83–84

"flooding", 155

food

    in clicker training, 29, 30, 40–41

    as lure, 34–35

    as reward, 14–15, 17

    schedule for giving, 183

free shaping, 30–31

front door. *See* doorways

frustration, digging and, 229

furniture, 45

G

games

    for exercise, 22–23

    as reward, 16

    see also tricks

Gentle Leader Headcollar, 198, *199*, 236

German Shepherd, *96*, *141*, *218*

Get Me a Bottle of Water trick, 101–103

Get the Mail/Newspaper trick, 80

Give Your Paw trick, 61

goals, setting, 46, 54–55

Go Find the Remote trick, 80–81

Go Get Mom trick, 98–99

Go Get the Phone trick, 81–82

Go Get Your Dish trick, 82–83

Go Get Your Leash trick, 79

Golden Retrievers, *24*, *41*, *57*, *82*, *101*, *120*, *127*, *136*, *141*, *169*, *218*, *237*

Go Left, Go Right trick, 103–104

Go Wake Up Daddy trick, 98

growling, 129

THE EVERYTHING SERIES!

BUSINESS & PERSONAL FINANCE

Everything® Budgeting Book
Everything® Business Planning Book
Everything® Coaching and Mentoring Book
Everything® Fundraising Book
Everything® Get Out of Debt Book
Everything® Grant Writing Book
Everything® Home-Based Business Book
Everything® Homebuying Book, 2nd Ed.
Everything® Homeselling Book, 2nd Ed.
Everything® Investing Book, 2nd Ed.
Everything® Landlording Book
Everything® Leadership Book
Everything® Managing People Book
Everything® Negotiating Book
Everything® Online Business Book
Everything® Personal Finance Book
Everything® Personal Finance in Your 20s
    and 30s Book
Everything® Project Management Book
Everything® Real Estate Investing Book
Everything® Robert's Rules Book, $7.95
Everything® Selling Book
Everything® Start Your Own Business Book
Everything® Wills & Estate Planning Book

COOKING

Everything® Barbecue Cookbook
Everything® Bartender's Book, $9.95
Everything® Chinese Cookbook
Everything® Cocktail Parties and Drinks
    Book
Everything® College Cookbook
Everything® Cookbook
Everything® Cooking for Two Cookbook
Everything® Diabetes Cookbook
Everything® Easy Gourmet Cookbook
Everything® Fondue Cookbook
Everything® Gluten-Free Cookbook

Everything® Grilling Cookbook
Everything® Healthy Meals in Minutes
    Cookbook
Everything® Holiday Cookbook
Everything® Indian Cookbook
Everything® Italian Cookbook
Everything® Low-Carb Cookbook
Everything® Low-Fat High-Flavor Cookbook
Everything® Low-Salt Cookbook
Everything® Meals for a Month Cookbook
Everything® Mediterranean Cookbook
Everything® Mexican Cookbook
Everything® One-Pot Cookbook
Everything® Pasta Cookbook
Everything® Quick Meals Cookbook
Everything® Slow Cooker Cookbook
Everything® Slow Cooking for a Crowd
    Cookbook
Everything® Soup Cookbook
Everything® Thai Cookbook
Everything® Vegetarian Cookbook
Everything® Wine Book, 2nd Ed.

CRAFT SERIES

Everything® Crafts—Baby Scrapbooking
Everything® Crafts—Bead Your Own Jewelry
Everything® Crafts—Create Your Own
    Greeting Cards
Everything® Crafts—Easy Projects
Everything® Crafts—Polymer Clay for
    Beginners
Everything® Crafts—Rubber Stamping
    Made Easy
Everything® Crafts—Wedding Decorations
    and Keepsakes

HEALTH

Everything® Alzheimer's Book
Everything® Diabetes Book
Everything® Health Guide to Controlling
    Anxiety

Everything® Hypnosis Book
Everything® Low Cholesterol Book
Everything® Massage Book
Everything® Menopause Book
Everything® Nutrition Book
Everything® Reflexology Book
Everything® Stress Management Book

HISTORY

Everything® American Government Book
Everything® American History Book
Everything® Civil War Book
Everything® Irish History & Heritage Book
Everything® Middle East Book

HOBBIES & GAMES

Everything® Blackjack Strategy Book
Everything® Brain Strain Book, $9.95
Everything® Bridge Book
Everything® Candlemaking Book
Everything® Card Games Book
Everything® Card Tricks Book, $9.95
Everything® Cartooning Book
Everything® Casino Gambling Book, 2nd Ed.
Everything® Chess Basics Book
Everything® Craps Strategy Book
Everything® Crossword and Puzzle Book
Everything® Crossword Challenge Book
Everything® Cryptograms Book, $9.95
Everything® Digital Photography Book
Everything® Drawing Book
Everything® Easy Crosswords Book
Everything® Family Tree Book, 2nd Ed.
Everything® Games Book, 2nd Ed.
Everything® Knitting Book
Everything® Knots Book
Everything® Photography Book
Everything® Poker Strategy Book
Everything® Pool & Billiards Book
Everything® Quilting Book
Everything® Scrapbooking Book

All Everything® books are priced at $12.95 or $14.95, unless otherwise stated. Prices subject to change without notice.

Everything® Sewing Book
Everything® Test Your IQ Book, $9.95
Everything® Travel Crosswords Book, $9.95
Everything® Woodworking Book
Everything® Word Games Challenge Book
Everything® Word Search Book

HOME IMPROVEMENT

Everything® Feng Shui Book
Everything® Feng Shui Decluttering Book,
$9.95
Everything® Fix-It Book
Everything® Homebuilding Book
Everything® Lawn Care Book
Everything® Organize Your Home Book

EVERYTHING®
KIDS' BOOKS

All titles are $6.95

Everything® Kids' Animal Puzzle & Activity
Book
Everything® Kids' Baseball Book, 3rd Ed.
Everything® Kids' Bible Trivia Book
Everything® Kids' Bugs Book
Everything® Kids' Christmas Puzzle
& Activity Book
Everything® Kids' Cookbook
Everything® Kids' Crazy Puzzles Book
Everything® Kids' Dinosaurs Book
Everything® Kids' Gross Jokes Book
Everything® Kids' Gross Puzzle and
Activity Book
Everything® Kids' Halloween Puzzle
& Activity Book
Everything® Kids' Hidden Pictures Book
Everything® Kids' Joke Book
Everything® Kids' Knock Knock Book
Everything® Kids' Math Puzzles Book
Everything® Kids' Mazes Book
Everything® Kids' Money Book
Everything® Kids' Nature Book
Everything® Kids' Puzzle Book
Everything® Kids' Riddles & Brain Teasers Book
Everything® Kids' Science Experiments Book
Everything® Kids' Sharks Book
Everything® Kids' Soccer Book
Everything® Kids' Travel Activity Book

KIDS' STORY BOOKS

Everything® Fairy Tales Book

LANGUAGE

Everything® Conversational Japanese Book
(with CD), $19.95
Everything® French Phrase Book, $9.95
Everything® French Verb Book, $9.95
Everything® Inglés Book
Everything® Learning French Book
Everything® Learning German Book
Everything® Learning Italian Book
Everything® Learning Latin Book
Everything® Learning Spanish Book
Everything® Sign Language Book
Everything® Spanish Grammar Book
Everything® Spanish Practice Book
(with CD), $19.95
Everything® Spanish Phrase Book, $9.95
Everything® Spanish Verb Book, $9.95

MUSIC

Everything® Drums Book (with CD), $19.95
Everything® Guitar Book
Everything® Home Recording Book
Everything® Playing Piano and Keyboards
Book
Everything® Reading Music Book (with CD),
$19.95
Everything® Rock & Blues Guitar Book
(with CD), $19.95
Everything® Songwriting Book

NEW AGE

Everything® Astrology Book, 2nd Ed.
Everything® Dreams Book, 2nd Ed.
Everything® Ghost Book
Everything® Love Signs Book, $9.95
Everything® Numerology Book
Everything® Paganism Book
Everything® Palmistry Book
Everything® Psychic Book
Everything® Reiki Book
Everything® Tarot Book
Everything® Wicca and Witchcraft Book

PARENTING

Everything® Baby Names Book
Everything® Baby Shower Book
Everything® Baby's First Food Book
Everything® Baby's First Year Book
Everything® Birthing Book
Everything® Breastfeeding Book
Everything® Father-to-Be Book
Everything® Father's First Year Book
Everything® Get Ready for Baby Book
Everything® Get Your Baby to Sleep Book,
$9.95
Everything® Getting Pregnant Book
Everything® Homeschooling Book
Everything® Mother's First Year Book
Everything® Parent's Guide to Children
and Divorce
Everything® Parent's Guide to Children
with ADD/ADHD
Everything® Parent's Guide to Children
with Asperger's Syndrome
Everything® Parent's Guide to Children
with Autism
Everything® Parent's Guide to Children with
Bipolar Disorder
Everything® Parent's Guide to Children
with Dyslexia
Everything® Parent's Guide to Positive
Discipline
Everything® Parent's Guide to Raising a
Successful Child
Everything® Parent's Guide to Tantrums
Everything® Parent's Guide to the Overweight
Child
Everything® Parent's Guide to the Strong-
Willed Child
Everything® Parenting a Teenager Book
Everything® Potty Training Book, $9.95
Everything® Pregnancy Book, 2nd Ed.
Everything® Pregnancy Fitness Book
Everything® Pregnancy Nutrition Book
Everything® Pregnancy Organizer, $15.00
Everything® Toddler Book
Everything® Tween Book
Everything® Twins, Triplets, and More Book

All Everything® books are priced at $12.95 or $14.95, unless otherwise stated. Prices subject to change without notice.

PETS

Everything® Cat Book
Everything® Dachshund Book
Everything® Dog Book
Everything® Dog Health Book
Everything® Dog Training and Tricks Book
Everything® German Shepherd Book
Everything® Golden Retriever Book
Everything® Horse Book
Everything® Horseback Riding Book
Everything® Labrador Retriever Book
Everything® Poodle Book
Everything® Pug Book
Everything® Puppy Book
Everything® Rottweiler Book
Everything® Small Dogs Book
Everything® Tropical Fish Book
Everything® Yorkshire Terrier Book

REFERENCE

Everything® Car Care Book
Everything® Classical Mythology Book
Everything® Computer Book
Everything® Divorce Book
Everything® Einstein Book
Everything® Etiquette Book, 2nd Ed.
Everything® Inventions and Patents Book
Everything® Mafia Book
Everything® Philosophy Book
Everything® Psychology Book
Everything® Shakespeare Book

RELIGION

Everything® Angels Book
Everything® Bible Book
Everything® Buddhism Book
Everything® Catholicism Book
Everything® Christianity Book
Everything® Jewish History & Heritage Book
Everything® Judaism Book
Everything® Koran Book
Everything® Prayer Book
Everything® Saints Book

Everything® Torah Book
Everything® Understanding Islam Book
Everything® World's Religions Book
Everything® Zen Book

SCHOOL & CAREERS

Everything® Alternative Careers Book
Everything® College Survival Book, 2nd Ed.
Everything® Cover Letter Book, 2nd Ed.
Everything® Get-a-Job Book
Everything® Guide to Starting and Running
   a Restaurant
Everything® Job Interview Book
Everything® New Teacher Book
Everything® Online Job Search Book
Everything® Paying for College Book
Everything® Practice Interview Book
Everything® Resume Book, 2nd Ed.
Everything® Study Book

SELF-HELP

Everything® Dating Book, 2nd Ed.
Everything® Great Sex Book
Everything® Kama Sutra Book
Everything® Self-Esteem Book

SPORTS & FITNESS

Everything® Fishing Book
Everything® Golf Instruction Book
Everything® Pilates Book
Everything® Running Book
Everything® Total Fitness Book
Everything® Weight Training Book
Everything® Yoga Book

TRAVEL

Everything® Family Guide to Hawaii
Everything® Family Guide to Las Vegas,
   2nd Ed.
Everything® Family Guide to New York City,
   2nd Ed.
Everything® Family Guide to RV Travel &
   Campgrounds

Everything® Family Guide to the Walt Disney
   World Resort®, Universal Studios®,
   and Greater Orlando, 4th Ed.
Everything® Family Guide to Cruise Vacations
Everything® Family Guide to the Caribbean
Everything® Family Guide to Washington
   D.C., 2nd Ed.
Everything® Guide to New England
Everything® Travel Guide to the Disneyland
   Resort®, California Adventure®,
   Universal Studios®, and the
   Anaheim Area

WEDDINGS

Everything® Bachelorette Party Book, $9.95
Everything® Bridesmaid Book, $9.95
Everything® Elopement Book, $9.95
Everything® Father of the Bride Book, $9.95
Everything® Groom Book, $9.95
Everything® Mother of the Bride Book, $9.95
Everything® Outdoor Wedding Book
Everything® Wedding Book, 3rd Ed.
Everything® Wedding Checklist, $9.95
Everything® Wedding Etiquette Book, $9.95
Everything® Wedding Organizer, $15.00
Everything® Wedding Shower Book, $9.95
Everything® Wedding Vows Book, $9.95
Everything® Weddings on a Budget Book,
   $9.95

WRITING

Everything® Creative Writing Book
Everything® Get Published Book
Everything® Grammar and Style Book
Everything® Guide to Writing a Book Proposal
Everything® Guide to Writing a Novel
Everything® Guide to Writing Children's Books
Everything® Guide to Writing Research Papers
Everything® Screenwriting Book
Everything® Writing Poetry Book
Everything® Writing Well Book